RÉSUMÉS, COVER LETTERS, & INTERVIEWING

Setting the Stage for Success

Clifford W. Eischen

Fresno City College

Lynn A. Eischen

Principal, Eischen Professional Résumé Service

South-Western College Publishing
Thomson Learning™

Australia • Canada • Denmark • Japan • Mexico • New Zealand • Phillipines
Puerto Rico • Singapore • South Africa • Spain • United Kingdom • United States

Publisher: Dave Shaut
Acquisitions Editor: Pamela M. Person
Developmental Editor: Katherine Pruitt-Schenck
Marketing Manager: Sarah J. Woelfel
Production Editor: Tamborah E. Moore
Manufacturing Coordinator: Dana Began Schwartz
Production House: Trejo Production
Printer: West Group

COPYRIGHT ©2000 by South-Western College Publishing
A Division of Thomson Learning

The Thomson Learning logo is a registered trademark used herein under license.
Printed in the United States of America
4 5 02 01

For more information contact South-Western College Publishing, 5191 Natorp Boulevard, Mason,
Ohio, 45040 or find us on the Internet at http://www.swcollege.com

All Rights Reserved. No part of this work covered by the copyright hereon may be reproduced or
used in any form or by any means—graphic, electronic, or mechanical, including photocopying,
recording, taping, or information storage and retrieval systems—without the written permission of
the publisher.

**You can request permission to use material from this text through the following phone and fax
numbers: telephone: 1-800-730-2214; fax: 1-800-730-2215
Or you can visit our web site at http://www.thomsonrights.com**

Library of Congress Cataloging-in-Publication Data
Eischen, Clifford W.
   Resumes, cover letters & interviewing : setting the stage for success / Clifford W. Eischen,
Lynn A. Eischen.
      p. cm
   Includes bibliographical references.
   ISBN 0-324-01404-X (alk. paper)
   1. Résumés (Employment)   2. Cover letters.   3. Employment interviewing.   I. Eischen, Lynn A.
II. Title.   III. Title: Resumes, cover letters, and interviewing.
   HF5383.E424   2000
   650.14--dc21   99-23751

*To our parents, Joseph F. and Emily E. Eischen
and Arthur C. and Alice L. Koller, who were
children of immigrants with meager resources
and limited education, but whose achievements
in the face of economic adversity proved to be a
standard for all of their offspring.*

*To our children, Drew, Todd, Kyle, Kathy, and
Chad who will now raise the bar even higher.*

P R E F A C E

More than 45 years of combined experience have made us into a knowledgeable and unique résumé team. Since 1972, we have prepared résumés professionally in a firm located in Fresno, California. In addition, Cliff has taught résumé writing at the community college level for more than 30 years. Our many years of teaching students to prepare résumés and cover letters, and assisting them with interviewing techniques have resulted in this text. We have honed our résumé writing and career coaching skills from a multitude of professional sources and attendance at seminars provided by the Professional Association of Résumé Writers and National Résumé Writers Association. We are members of these organizations and are certified by them.

The material in this text takes a step-by-step approach to the development of professional résumés and career marketing materials. Résumé writing is not difficult; however, it does take considerable time and some word processing skills to create attention-getting résumés. The key to every good résumé is research, attractive layout, and numerous rewrites. This book should help you develop a résumé that you will proudly show to prospective employers. It will teach you how to prepare résumés for scanning, e-mailing, and faxing. We have provided numerous examples of résumés, cover letters, letters of recommendation, follow-up letters, salary history and reference pages, answers to interview questions, and samples of business skills that may be included in a résumé.

Just as technology has changed how we communicate, so have résumés changed. We now post résumés on the Internet, send them via e-mail and fax, and sometimes provide a résumé on a floppy disk or even a video demonstrating the candidate's best attributes. Change will continue and who is to say that in the next five years we won't be placing résumés on a credit-card-sized piece of plastic containing a magnetic strip or embedded chip. For now, the vehicle of choice for job seekers and employers is the well written, professional résumé. In this text we have simplified this process for you and wish you well as you embark on your career search using the tools and strategies found in this publication.

In writing this text we are deeply indebted and thankful for the contributions, editing, and encouragement provided by the following colleagues. This project would never have come to fruition without their assistance and support.

Sherian Eckenrod
Gigi Hill
Jack Hill
Cary Jones

Connie Kendrick-Murphy
Marlene Putnam
Robin Rosenthal
Alice Stone

We would also like to thank the reviewers who provided outstanding feedback on shaping the goals and purposes of this text. They include: William B. Chapel, Michigan Technological University; Roger N. Conaway, The University of Texas at Tyler; Martha Kuchar, Roanoke College; and Jim Rucker, Fort Hays State University.

Lastly, thanks to the staff at South-Western College Publishing for helping bring this project from ideas and strategies to a bound text: Pamela Person, Acquisitions Editor; Katherine Pruitt-Schenck, Developmental Editor; Tamborah Moore, Production Editor; Lynn Mills, Assistant; and Sarah Woelfel, Marketing Manager.

— *Lynn and Cliff Eischen*

ENHANCE YOUR COURSE WITH THESE OUTSTANDING RESOURCES

HOW 8: Handbook for Office Workers.

(0 538 86319 6)

By Lyn Clark and James Clark

This handbook is the most comprehensive reference manual available for writing, formatting, and transmitting business documents. It is designed to assist office professionals and business writers in preparing successful written business communications. Completely updated, it reflects the most current use of technology in the office, including e-mail and the Internet.

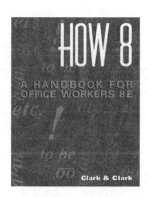

The Professional Writer's Electronic Resource (PoWER) CD-ROM.

(0-538-87895-9)

By Mary Ellen Guffey, Lyn Clark, and James Clark

This on-line reference and interactive study guide reviews and reinforces grammar, spelling, punctuation, mechanics, and usage in all forms of communication. The software includes pretests, posttests, examples, lessons, and exercises.

Business Communications, the Real World, and Your Career.

(0-324-01426-0)

By James Sequin

This brief text teaches students how to use the business communication skills they learn in college to obtain the career they want and advance professionally. It is a perfect supplement to any business communication course or for instructors teaching in any discipline who want to show their students how to apply skills from their coursework in their professional lives. Special attention is given to lifelong learning and career development, including networking and communications skill building.

Start Now. Succeed Later: Making College Count for Career Search Success.
By Pat O'Brien, (0-324-01540-2)

This highly approachable, graphics-intensive book helps students to understand what they need to do throughout their college experience to build the skills necessary to ultimately achieve success in the job interview process. Highlighted are key skills that students should begin building now, through academics, extra-curricular activities, and relevant work experience, to maximize their career opportunities. Combining clear and immediate directions on developing these skills with examples and interviews with recruiting executives, this text gives students the tools they need to turn their college experiences into future job success.

Wired Résumés. http://www.wired-resumes.com By Tim Krause

<Wired Resumes>

Wired Résumés is the first and only Web site that allows instructors to walk students through the process of creating a professional quality on-line resume—and *Wired Résumés Guide* assures success for all.

Wired Résumés Guide. http://www.wired-resumes.com
(0-324-01538-0) By Tim Krause

Tim Krause, co-director of Business Writing at Purdue University, contributor to *Business Communication Quarterly*, and electronic communication specialist with Cargill Industries, gives you and your students all the help you need to successfully navigate the Wired **Résumés** Web site regardless of skill or experience level.

Career Strategies. (0-324-01403-1) By Thomas Clark
This workbook is designed to take the reader through the process of assesssing skills and talents, developing a networking data bank, preparing job search marketing tools, and answering interview questions effectively.

The Business Communicator: An Interactive CD Series.
By Michael Netzley (0-324-02234-4)

This series of interactive, technology-based learning tools focus on key business communication issues that can be enhanced by CD-ROM delivery. This portion of the series consists of modules including organizing a message, document design, visual presentations, and presenting financial information. Technology-based delivery enhances understanding of the material through multimedia and highly interactive lessons, examples, and skill checks.

C O N T E N T S

LISTING OF RÉSUMÉS, COVER LETTERS, AND EXAMPLES

Resumes

Cover Letters

Additional Examples

RÉSUMÉS, COVER LETTERS, & INTERVIEWING

Setting the Stage for Success

Setting the Stage

THE SCREENING PROCESS: MAKING THE CUT

The purpose of a résumé is to allow the potential employer the opportunity to find out a lot about you in a few minutes, maybe even seconds, to determine if he/she would like to meet you in person. This determination will often be made on the basis of one or two sheets of paper—the résumé and cover letter that you have submitted to an employer via mail, fax, or e-mail.

The process is similar to one that is used when we first meet others. We look at them, their clothes, posture, smile, laugh, eyes, etc., and then decide whether we would like to get to know them better. Our evaluation of them is based upon whether the qualities they possess are similar to those that we value. In other words, if the first time we see someone we note that they have a pleasant smile, laugh easily, and don't smoke, we might want to get to know them better, especially if we like people who are positive, have a good sense of humor and are non-smokers. Well, employers do the same thing. They look for *qualities that you have that are valued in their businesses*. The characteristics they value are usually a positive attitude, related work experience, formal education, and training in areas where they have a specific need, such as welding, word processing, hair styling, filing, customer service, etc. If they see that you have these skills, they will probably want to meet with you and conduct an interview to see if you are someone they want to get to know even better and consider for possible employment in their firm.

But be aware, it is not just the skills listed on your résumé that are important. It is much more than the words you place on the résumé page or cover letter that are important. The *appearance* of the résumé page and cover letter is critical. When you see a fascinating person across the room at a party, *initially it is their image or appearance* that catches your eye and makes them interesting. The qualities that attract you to them are sometimes definable and sometimes not. However, in a résumé we can usually identify the characteristics that make the résumé appealing to the reader.

APPEARANCE IS CRITICAL

In a résumé *appearance is critical.* Initially, your résumé's appearance will have the greatest impact on the reader/employer. The paper that you choose (quality and color), the placement on the paper (whether it's centered), the typeface and size used, spelling and punctuation, headings used, length of previous jobs, communication skills (choice of words and use of key words), and organization will all be reviewed by the reader. Some employers will look for a flaw to screen out candidates who are not careful in one of the areas mentioned above. After the initial impression and upon reading the cover letter and résumé (and this will only occur if the reader likes what he/she has initially seen), the reader will begin to look at the organization of your material, your skills, experience, and education. And in the case of the cover letter, the *tone* of your letter, meaning its attitude and whether it is positive, will be the primary focus. From that first impression an employer will decide whether they want to get to know you better—have a first date/interview you.

THINGS YOU MUST DO

Because a professional appearance is critical, it is appropriate to do the following:

1. Prepare your résumé on a word processor (computer) using a laser or ink-jet printer (the printed typeface should be clean and precise, not fuzzy). The reason for using a word processor is so that your résumé can be modified easily. Often you will need to modify it when applying for a specific position. Also you may think of some activity at a later time that you want to include. Therefore, it is essential to have your résumé stored on disk for later modification.
2. The written material should appear centered on the page—both vertically and horizontally. It doesn't have to be measured precisely, simply look centered when viewed by the naked eye.
3. Use the spell-checker feature of the word processing program. Remember, every technical or business product name (like Xerox), plus the names of individuals, should be double-checked for accuracy as the spell-checker feature of most software programs will not spotlight misspellings in these types of words.
4. Have a friend, maybe two, who has a formal education and/or a college degree proofread your résumé.
5. Complete the résumé several days before you need it. Doing it at midnight the day before you have an 8 A.M. interview often results in shoddy work.
6. The paper used for a résumé should be light gray, ivory, or white; 24 pound classic laid stock.

RÉSUMÉ EXAMPLES

To illustrate how important appearance is, look at Figures 1 and 2 on the following pages. Figures 1 and 2 have identical written text (are the same résumé); however, the formatting (appearance) of Figure 1 is very professional in appearance, while Figure 2 is unacceptable because of improper spacing, centering, and layout. Remember *how you present your written material is as important as what you write.* The résumé represents you at your best; therefore, look your best.

Figure 1 Professional Appearance

Rafael E. Cortez

5559 E. Spruce Ave.
Clovis, CA 93611
(559) 845-9621

OBJECTIVE   *Administrative Assistant Position with Orange School District*

QUALIFICATIONS
- Associate Degree and Certificate in Business Office Occupations.
- Three years' experience in retail customer service and internship in educational administrative office.
- Excellent word processing skills–MS Word and WordPerfect.
- Bilingual–read, write, and speak fluent Spanish.
- Experience as leader of college organization.
- Office skills include: 10-key by touch, type 48 WPM, and work well on team projects.
- Industrious and dependable–missed only one school day in the last year.
- Quick learner–able to grasp instructions accurately and complete tasks as requested.

EDUCATION   *Associate Degree in Business Office Occupations–Administrative Assistant Emphasis*
Certificate granted, Administrative Assistant Program
Fresno City College, Fresno, CA, 1998
Completed program with a 3.4 GPA.

EMPLOYMENT   *Internship*   Spring, 1998
Washington Union High School, Easton, CA
- Completed 5-month internship in busy administrative office.
- Prepared correspondence and newsletter using MS Word.
- Assisted in data entry, scheduling appointments, routing phone messages on multi-line telephone system.
- Translated for Spanish-speaking parents.
- Performed filing tasks–alphabetical and numerical.

Customer Service / Sales Associate (part-time)   1996 - Present
Bargain Mart, Fresno, CA
- Assist customers with merchandise and ring up sales.
- Stock shelves and price merchandise.
- Received 3 salary increases while employed at this busy store.
- Asked to assume full-time position.

Figure 2 Poor Appearance

Rafael E. Cortez
5559 E. Spruce Ave.
Clovis, CA 93611
(559) 845-9621

OBJECTIVE	Administrative Assistant Position with Orange School District.
QUALIFICATIONS	Associate Degree and Certificate in Business Office occupations.
	Three years' experience in retail customer service and internship in educational administrative office.
	Excellent word processing skills–MS Word and WordPerfect.
	Bilingual–read, write, and speak fluent Spanish.
	Experience as leader of college organization.
	Office skills include: 10-key by touch, type 48 WPM, and work well on team projects.
	Industrious and dependable–missed only one school day in the last year.
	Quick learner–able to grasp instructions accurately and complete tasks as requested.
EDUCATION	Associate Degree in Business Office Occupations–Administrative Assistant Emphasis
	Certificate granted, Administrative Assistant Program
	Fresno City College, Fresno, CA, 1998
	Completed program with a 3.4 GPA.
EMPLOYMENT	Internship, Spring, 1998
	Washington Union High School, Easton, CA
	Completed 5-month internship in busy administrative office.
	Prepared correspondence and newsletter using MS Word.
	Assisted in data entry, scheduling appointments, routing phone messages on multi-line telephone system.
	Translated for Spanish speaking parents.
	Performed filing tasks–alphabetical and numerical.
	Customer Service / Sales Associate (part-time) 1996-Present
	Bargain Mart, Fresno, CA
	Assist customers with merchandise and ring up sales.
	Stock shelves and price merchandise.
	Received 3 salary increases while employed at this busy store.
	Asked to assume full time position.

Practice Your Skills

Your Name
Your Address

OBJECTIVE

QUALIFICATIONS

EDUCATION

EMPLOYMENT

CHAPTER 2

The Audition: Establish Your Qualifications

YOUR STRENGTHS

Most probably your strengths will be your education, employment, professional achievements and affiliations, honors, awards, military experience, leadership training, languages, computer literacy, and special projects that you have completed. At the end of this chapter you will find an exercise which will help you list your strengths. Be sure to complete the exercise *after* reading the following paragraphs; it will make writing your résumé a lot easier—trust us.

EDUCATION

In most instances education will be one of your strengths. The focus for education in your résumé is twofold: 1) to list the degree/s, certificate/s, and honors that you have received during your formal education, and 2) to state the specific skills and knowledge you have acquired from the educational program/s that you have completed. Place these in the designated area on the Exercise I form at the end of this chapter.

EMPLOYMENT

No doubt you have worked in either part-time or full-time positions during high school and college. It is essential that you list your employment, even if it is not related to the job you are currently seeking and was unpaid. Nearly everyone has worked for someone else—with or without compensation. If this is not the case, immediately go to a teacher, career center, counselor, or mentor and find out how to get some OJT (on-the-job training) in your community. It is necessary that you have work experience. The experience may be paid or volunteer. Even if the work may be for only a few hours a week, gain some experience in a job close to the one that you eventually want to obtain. Place all your employment experience in the designated area on the Exercise I form.

SPECIAL PROJECTS

Ask yourself if you have completed any of the following at work or at school:

1. Initiated a project. Some examples: reorganized the stockroom, developed a safety program for those in your place of employment, suggested a new form that would save time, or developed a method to reduce costs.
2. Developed time-saving methods. Some examples: while delivering customer orders, picked up merchandise from suppliers, or devised a short-cut to reduce the time it takes to weld a cabinet.
3. Taken a leadership role. Some examples: became an officer in a student organization, agreed to serve as chairperson for the United Givers Plan, or was selected by your teacher to make a presentation to businesses in the community.
4. Saved your employer money: An example: suggested a way to ship goods that provided a cost saving over current shipping costs.
5. Stood out among your peers. Some examples: had the highest sales for a three-month period, assisted a customer who later complimented you in a letter to your employer, or received an earlier-than-expected pay increase.

List the special projects that you have completed on the Exercise I form.

HONORS/AWARDS

If your school, peers, employer, or community have honored you, it is special. Thus, if you made the Dean's List at your college, graduated in the top 25 percent of your class or program, received a bonus at work, were asked to become a team leader, were selected as lead person for some project, or were designated as employee or student of the month, it is a big deal and should be noted on your résumé.

PROFESSIONAL AND COMMUNITY ORGANIZATIONS

It is important to identify relevant professional and community groups of which you are a member. These can be school or college-affiliated chapters of these organizations. Why are these affiliations important? They show that you are committed to your career choice and desire to become more knowledgeable through membership in and attendance at trade or professional meetings. Some examples of professional organizations: The American Paralegal Association and the American Student Paralegal Association; Alpha Gamma Sigma; and Phi Beta Lambda. Labor unions sometimes provide education and training for student members. If you have participated in an apprenticeship program, be sure to list it. Being a member of a community group such as Public Television, Toastmasters, or The Heart Association is also positive and should be identified on your résumé. It is even more significant if you have taken an active leadership role, chaired a committee, or served as an officer in any professional organization. List any such memberships and activities on the Exercise I form.

COMPUTER LITERACY

Today, everyone needs to be computer literate. It is essential that you state your computer and software skills on your résumé. You should identify the operating systems with which you are familiar. Basically, there are two: Windows 95/98 and Apple/Macintosh operating systems. There are some others that are used by computer pros, and if you know how to use them, list them also. If you are applying for an accounts receivable position it would be essential to indicate that you have a knowledge of bookkeeping/accounting software, such as Excel, Peachtree, Lotus 1-2-3, Quick Books, etc. The more programs you know, the more valuable you are to an employer. To list a program doesn't mean you have to know every aspect of the program. Being familiar with its major functions is OK. If you have worked in an office that used customized software for that particular industry, go ahead and list this software—it shows you are adaptable and can learn new programs quickly. If you have acquired skills in programming, repairing, networking, assembling, or troubleshooting computers, list these also.

LANGUAGES AND CULTURE

Besides slang, what languages do you speak? If there are significant numbers of Laotians in your community and you speak Lao, it is a plus. Put it on your résumé—it may just be the positive factor that gives you the edge in your job search so that you get the position you want. In addition to languages, you may have lived in a country or territory that provided you with special knowledge of a culture or practices within that country. An example would be someone who spent five years living in Mexico and working for an airline. If this individual applies for a position with an airline that has routes to Mexico, it would be beneficial to state that you have knowledge of the language, airline industry, and cultural practices of this country.

GOVERNMENT SERVICE

If you have been a member of the Job or Peace Corps, served in the military, or traveled extensively, you may have acquired some skills or knowledge that would be valuable to an employer. The key to determining whether to list a Job Corps, military, or travel background is whether the knowledge and skills you acquired are *relevant* to the position for which you are applying.

EXERCISE I

Show Me Your Qualifications: An Initial Listing

1. Place the appropriate answers to the material discussed in the preceding paragraphs on the lines below.

   #### A. Education
   1. List degrees, certificates, credentials, licenses, and GPA.

   _____

   _____

   _____

   _____

   2. Indicate skills acquired. Some examples: (skills for a hair stylist) hair styling, coloring, cutting, and sterilization of implements; (skills for a receptionist) use of multi-line phone system, experience in scheduling appointments, data entry, and greeting customers; (skills for an electrician) pulling wire, knowledge of circuitry and electrical controls, ability to utilize CAD drawings for initial installations, and understand VFD applications and installation.

      Nearly every occupation and industry has a specific set of skills. By using a college catalog which contains skill sets taught in each course, checking *The Dictionary of Occupational Titles*, to be found in most career centers, or reviewing job descriptions and advertisements, you should determine the skills that are appropriate for the desired occupation and include those that are most important in that occupation on the résumé.

      Below are some common skills found in business and computer science:

Keyboarding/Typing	Windows/Macintosh
Statistical Typing	Word Processing
10-Key by Touch	Programming Languages
Bank Reconciliation	Computer Programs
Bookkeeping	Networking Skills
Computer Bookkeeping	Internet Knowledge
General Ledger	Homepage Creation
Payroll	Writing Skills
Accounts Payable	Proficient Use of Grammar
Accounts Receivable	Foreign Languages
Auditing	Persuasive People Skills
Tax Return Preparation	Dependable/Flexible
Financial Planning	Diplomatic/Patient
Cost Analysis	Team Player
Medical Terminology	Leadership Ability
Legal Terminology	Organizational Skills
Excellent Speller	Self-Directed
Office Correspondence	Manage Time Effectively
Machine Dictation	Problem Solver
Shorthand/Transcription	Able to Motivate Others
Computer Literate	Decisive/Analytical

Now list your skills below:

_____

_____

_____

_____

_____

_____

_____

_____

B. Employment

1. List employers (paid or volunteer) with *most recent first.* List:
   a. employers, with accurately spelled business name as found in the telephone directory
   b. give dates of employment—beginning and ending
   c. your job title
   d. what you did and the skills used or acquired on the job
   e. training given and others whom you trained
   f. promotions received—give job titles from initial position to final/current position
   g. responsibilities, examples would be: opening/closing store, making bank deposits, authorizing overtime, buying new equipment, etc.
   h. evaluations—comments and ratings on any formal evaluations

_____

_____

_____

_____

_____

_____

_____

_____

_____

_____

_____

_____

C. Special Projects. Refer to the material described earlier in the chapter for information on what to place in this area.

_____

_____

_____

_____

_____

_____

_____

D. Honors or Awards. State the honors and awards you have received at school, work, in the community, or in the military. These can be for attendance, sports, tutoring other students—any type of recognition.

_____

_____

_____

_____

E. Professional and Community Organizations. List the professional (work-related), community, and school-related organizations of which you are or have been a member. Also list any offices held, projects completed for these organizations, or special recognition or awards you received.

_____

_____

_____

_____

F. Computer Literacy. Indicate the following:
1. Type of computer systems you have operated (Windows or Apple)
2. Programs that you operate
3. Programming skills
4. Hardware skills—can you repair or upgrade a computer?
5. Networking knowledge
6. Internet and e-mail skills

_____

_____

_____

_____

_____

G. Languages. Indicate any language with which you are familiar. Give your level of skill (conversational, studied 2 years, fluent) and whether you can read, write, and speak the language.

_____

_____

_____

H. Government Service. State the type of government service that you have had—paid or volunteer is OK. You may have already listed this under employment. If not, state it here and provide the same information as you would for a job.

_____

_____

_____

Congratulations on completing Exercise I. You have just taken a huge step in the writing of your résumé. Feel free to go back and add to items that you listed. You probably will need to come back to this form two or three times before you remember most of the relevant items for each category.

Now, we urge you to ask your parents, brother, sister, or close friend to look at this exercise and see if they fully understand each of the accomplishments/activities you listed, and also if they can suggest additional items to add to any of these categories.

The final step, if applicable, is to show it to your teacher. He/she may have some additional suggestions.

Showtime: Present Your Strengths

RÉSUMÉ FORMAT

The following is the suggested format for your résumé. It is the same format that was used in the sample résumé, Figure 1, Chapter 1.

First, the **heading** which will contain your *name, address, telephone number/s*, and *e-mail address* (if you have one). These are to be centered at the top of the page, beginning one inch below the top edge; an example is shown below:

MELVIN MURGATROY
1479 South Ocean Blvd.
Hollywood, CA 90019
(416) 897-2828
E-mail: mmurgatr@anyuniversity.edu

Next, you will place the word **objective** *or* **focus** in bold capitals at the left margin.

OBJECTIVE/FOCUS

Then,

QUALIFICATIONS

and the remaining sections as follows:

EDUCATION

EMPLOYMENT

SKILLS

ORGANIZATIONS AND ACTIVITIES

Now that you have an overview of the section headings that will appear on your résumé, we will examine each of the sections on an individual basis, provide examples, and discuss what goes in each of them and why.

OBJECTIVE/FOCUS/POWER STATEMENT

Yes, it is wise to have a specific *objective/focus* (job in mind). We like both words and use them interchangeably on résumés. The reason for an objective is that employers believe you should know the type of position on which you want to focus and think you would enjoy and in which you have developed skill sets. Employers believe that if you don't know the type of work that you want to do, you may only be with them a short time until something else catches your imagination. Employers recruit employees hoping that they will stay with them for a long time, as it is costly and time-consuming to train new employees.

An example of the objective section for someone who is seeking a position as an acetylene welder is:

OBJECTIVE   *POSITION AS AN ACETYLENE WELDER*

There may be some instances when you omit this section (objective/focus) to make your résumé appeal to a broader audience, but this is the exception. We recommend that most beginning job hunters state a specific job or general position for which they have been trained. You will have much better results if an objective is stated. Often it is simply stating the title of the position that has been advertised, listed on a job description sheet, or passed on to you by someone in the company to which you are applying. But the position should be one for which you are qualified.

You will note that when you state your objective/focus, it should be placed three spaces below the address and appear in bold and/or capital letters to easily bring the reader's attention to it.

You can enhance your objective/focus statement with what is termed a "power statement." A power statement indicates the position you desire and also states your most outstanding qualifications. An example is:

FOCUS   *SKILLED WELDER WITH ADVANCED OXYACETYLENE, MIG, TIG EXPERIENCE AND CERTIFICATION BY THE AMERICAN WELDING SOCIETY IS SEEKING CAREER POSITION*

Perhaps it is obvious why this is called a power statement. One can easily determine that the applicant has excellent skills in welding and received certification by a national society for that occupational group. Thus, by mentioning these strong skills in the objective/focus statement, it gets the reader/employer's attention and makes an immediate impact. You may recall that employers spend only a short time scanning résumés unless they see something that grabs their interest. The purpose of the power statement is to get their attention immediately so that they will want to look at the remainder of the résumé and then give you a call to see if you are as good in person as you appear to be in the résumé.

If you want your résumé to have broader application, another option is to omit the objective/focus section. Usually this is not recommended because it may appear that you don't have a sense of direction. However, if you are applying to a company that has several positions for which you believe you are qualified, you may not want to specify only one position. To continue with the example in the focus/power statement for the welder above, let's assume that the résumé was being submitted to a company that had positions open for a sheet metal fabricator, an acetylene welder, a shop maintenance worker, and a maintenance mechanic. If you submit a résumé with an objective/focus for the acetylene welder position, and the company has many well-qualified candidates and then fills that position with someone other than you, they probably would not consider you for the other three positions. Thus, in this instance, if you omit the objective/focus statement and your résumé contains skills that might qualify you for all four positions, it would be smart *not* to state a specific job—therefore, omit the objective/focus portion.

QUALIFICATIONS SUMMARY

The qualifications summary is the heart of the résumé and will be an overview of the major qualifications you possess. In this section your best qualifications are to be stated simply and concisely. To do this you will need to refer to Figure 1 in Chapter 1 and Exercise I in Chapter 2. We suggest that you remove the pages containing Figure 1 and Exercise I, and place them in front of you as you complete the remainder of the sections in your résumé.

In this section you are to take the *best*, but not all, qualifications you have going for you in education, employment, special projects, honors, organizations, computers, languages, and government service and then concisely list them in the qualifications portion of your résumé. This step can be easily accomplished and is critical to preparing a successful résumé. If there were *key words* used in a newspaper advertisement or job announcement indicating certain skills that were desired, it is essential that you use these key words in describing your qualifications. You are to place only the vital elements of your education, employment, etc. in the qualifications section.

A central idea to remember while completing your résumé and the qualifications section is that the most relevant/important information related to the position for which you are applying should appear *first*. Follow this guideline throughout the construction of your résumé. In addition to putting the most relevant material first, place the most *recent* experiences *first*.

In the qualifications section of Figure 1 (the résumé for Rafael Cortez), you will note that the first item listed is a degree in Business Office Occupations. This is probably the single most important qualification relating to his seeking an administrative assistant's position. Note that information regarding his degree is more fully detailed under the education section.

The next item in the qualifications sections indicates, "Three years' experience in retail customer service and internship in educational administrative office." This refers to his three years of experience as a Customer Service/Sales Associate at Bargain Mart and his internship at Washington Union High School—both are listed with more information under the employment section. This is significant for several reasons:

- It shows he held one job for several years.
- It indicates he has interacted with customers and peers successfully.
- He probably acquired some training in customer service which will be useful to future employers.
- He has some actual experience working in the administrative offices of a school.

The same concepts apply to the other items contained in the qualifications section. Many items appearing in the qualifications section are also listed later on the résumé with more detail given. Sometimes statements regarding accomplishments or characteristics that appear in the qualifications section are *not* given more detail in a separate section. For instance, in the example below the last item in the foodservice worker's qualifications section is, "Learn quickly and relate well to coworkers and management." This statement appears only in the qualifications section of this résumé because no additional details are necessary. In essence, the statement speaks for itself.

Here is an example of a résumé qualifications section for a foodservice worker (Cook in Training):

QUALIFICATIONS

- Associate Degree in Food and Nutrition.
- Two years of experience as Prep Cook with local restaurants; received "Employee of the Month" award, January, 1999.
- Trained in meat cutting, baking, use of seasonings, salad preparation, food & beverage purchasing, and food sanitation.
- Additional part-time experience (2 years) as retail sales clerk.
- Bilingual—read, write, and speak fluent Spanish.
- Learn quickly and relate well to coworkers and management.

Now it's your turn. In Exercise II which follows, place the pages containing the answers to Exercise I, Chapter 2, in front of you and select your most significant qualifications related to the position you are applying for, then place them in Exercise II on the next page.

EXERCISE II

QUALIFICATIONS

1. _____
_____
_____

2. _____
_____
_____

3. _____
_____
_____

4. _____
_____
_____

5. _____
_____
_____

6. _____
_____
_____

7. _____
_____
_____

8. _____
_____
_____

9. _____
_____
_____

EDUCATION

If you have just completed an educational program and have limited related employment experience, the next section will normally be education. However, if you have substantial employment or related experience, the employment section would appear next. Again, the principle is to put the *most important* (important in qualifying you for the job you are seeking) *sections closest to the top of the page.*

In the education section of the résumé state in the following order:

1. the degree, certificate, or program completed and your major course or field of study
2. the college attended and where located
3. date program was or will be completed
4. class ranking and/or GPA (grade point average) if above a 3.0 ("B" average)
5. any special awards, honors, or recognition.

An example of the education section for a Legal Office Administration major would be as follows:

EDUCATION   **Associate in Applied Science Degree, Legal Office Administration**
Heald College, School of Business, Oakland, CA, 1999
Graduated in top 10% of class
GPA = 3.82 within major
Recipient: "Outstanding Legal Office Administration Graduate Award"

Special Skills

Sometimes a special skills section might be inserted before the employment section and after education. This would be the case if the applicant just mentioned had special skills in Legal Office Administration that were not mentioned elsewhere.

For example:

LEGAL OFFICE SKILLS   *Competencies include:*
Software: WordPerfect, legal version 7.0
Fast Track Software
Proforma
Verdict
Calendaring, billing, filing, tables of authority, and tickler files

If you have a special skills section like the one above, it would normally be placed after the education section. Also, you might take the most significant parts of the skills section and place them in the qualifications section at the very top of the résumé, e.g.,

• Excellent legal word processing skills using WordPerfect Legal and Fast Track.

Professional Licenses and Certifications

Often those who have received licenses from a state agency need to indicate this in their résumés. Sometimes a certification is received from a professional association and is significant because it communicates to an employer that this applicant has passed a difficult testing program and received recognition as a certified specialist. Earlier in this chapter it was noted that a welder was certified by the American Welding Association. Certification or licensing by a state or national organization or agency is a strong selling point to a prospective employer. So if you have it, be sure to put it on your résumé. Place it under education or skills, unless you really want to bring attention to it, then it is best to have a separate heading that will really spotlight it (see example that follows).

The following licenses and certifications are listed for a dental back office applicant:

LICENSE & CERTIFICATIONS
- Idaho X-Ray License, issued January, 1999.
- Coronal Polish Certificate.
- Certified in Spanish Language, Intermediate Level Examination, 1999.

EMPLOYMENT

In most résumés the employment section will appear next. This is sometimes referred to as the *experience* or *employment history* section.

The items in an employment listing are:

1. job title—if it is part-time, say so—then state dates of employment (usually at the far right so that they can be easily viewed)
2. employer's name (use the firm name, not the manager's or your supervisor's name), city, and state
3. your responsibilities and achievements with this employer. Some *key things* prospective employers look for in this section are:
   A. whether you have long-term and continuous employment, as opposed to many jobs lasting only one, two or three months
   B. time gaps between employment (unaccounted-for time periods between employment create questions in an employer's mind)

Below is an employment section for someone seeking back office medical assisting employment.

EMPLOYMENT
Medical Assistant Internship, Back Office   Fall, 1999
Kenneth Yogata, M.D., Peoria, Illinois
- Assisted with minor surgery and patient examinations; also instructed patients regarding physical therapy.
- Additional activities included: recording patient's symptoms, medical history, and blood pressure; sanitizing examination rooms; and preparing trays for subsequent procedures.
- Offered part-time paid position upon completion of internship program.

MISCELLANEOUS RÉSUMÉ SECTIONS

Organizations and Activities

Those who are active in professional and community organizations tend to be people oriented—meaning they usually relate well to other people. Getting along with people may be the most important skill you possess. We all know individuals who are very talented and quite bright but have difficulty interacting with their peers, bosses, or customers. Substantial research indicates that *more employees lose their jobs because of poor human relations skills than for any other reason.* Employers want to know if you have been involved in social and professional groups because they believe this will make you a better team player.

There is another reason that employers react positively to your belonging to *professional* groups. Membership in professional groups often provides opportunities for increased technical knowledge, networking/leadership opportunities, and professional growth. In a nutshell, what this really means is that someone who is professionally active will be better informed about what is going on in their occupation/industry. They will probably receive a publication, attend professional meetings where workshops regarding the latest concepts and technology are discussed, and will regularly meet people at conferences who are excited and knowledgeable about this occupation and industry.

The following is an example of an organizations and activities section for a management trainee applicant desiring employment with a major fast-food chain.

ORGANIZATIONS/ACTIVITIES
- Member/Treasurer, Students in Free Enterprise (SIFE).
- Member of SIFE college team which placed first in state competition, third in International Competition, Kansas City, MO.
- Cheerleader 2 years; Head Cheerleader 1 year.
- Member, Fellowship of Christian Athletes.

Military, Job/Peace Corps

Usually military service is inserted under either employment or education if you acquired substantial training while serving in the military. The same would be true for the Job or Peace Corps. Place relevant experience, education, and skills acquired under those respective sections.

References

References should be placed on a separate sheet. An example is provided in Chapter 6. Chapter 6 also discusses salary history and when it is appropriate to include information regarding previous earnings.

CHAPTER 4

Showtime Essentials: Résumé Presentation

ATTRACTIVE APPEARANCE AND FORMAT

If you were going to sell your car, what would be your first step? Would it be to make the car look as good as possible by washing and detailing it? Well, the same principle applies to selling you and your talents. The résumé is designed to market you to a prospective employer, resulting in your being called for an interview. The way to do that is to present a résumé that is professional in appearance. It is not difficult to do this in an age of word processors and laser printers. With very little effort the major word processing programs, MS Word and WordPerfect, will help you look good on paper if you use the features available in these programs. If you don't have a personal computer at home, try your public library or computer lab at the community college.

There are features present on the major software programs that will assist you to:

- Automatically center text horizontally and vertically (use block feature and then use centering feature).
- Place text in *italics*, **bold**, or <u>underline</u> (use block feature and then text feature).
- Use bullets (like those that appear at the left margin) or character/symbol sets (also ✔, ★, ➔, and ⇨) to emphasize and bring attention to important material on your résumé.
- Place material (such as dates of employment) adjacent to the right margin—known as the "flush right" or "align right" feature.
- Use a horizontal line to separate sections of the résumé. Note that the first résumé example separated the address from the objective with two horizontal lines (Figure 1, Chapter 1).

The use of these features adds greatly to the attractiveness of your résumé; so does the absence of spelling and grammatical errors (see the Error Free section in this chapter). Both major software programs possess features which check the spelling of *most* words, but not all—remember that company names won't be checked. These programs also have tools which assist in correcting punctuation and grammatical errors.

Another way to make your résumé more attractive is to use substantial "white space." This term means to leave the areas white or blank before and after text material. Maybe you have seen a large company use an entire page in a newspaper for an advertisement, and then place only ONE WORD on the page. Everyone who looks at that page will be drawn to that one word—usually a company or product name. White space around text causes one to focus on the text. The more white space you place around a section of your résumé, the greater the reader's focus.

The following example taken from the qualifications section in Figures 1 and 2, Chapter 1, illustrates this concept. Note how the achievements stand out in the first example when a line of white space is placed before and between the bulleted items.

QUALIFICATIONS

- Associate Degree and Certificate in Business Office Occupations.

- Three years' experience in retail customer service and internship in educational administrative office.

- Excellent word processing skills—MS Word and WordPerfect.

- Bilingual—read, write, and speak fluent Spanish.

- Experience as leader of college organization.

- Office skills include: 10-key by touch, type 48 WPM, and work well on team projects.

- Industrious and dependable—missed only one school day in the last year.

- Quick learner—able to grasp instructions accurately and complete tasks as requested.

QUALIFICATIONS

- Associate Degree and Certificate in Business Office Occupations.
- Three years' experience in retail customer service and internship in educational administrative office.
- Excellent word processing skills—MS Word and WordPerfect.
- Bilingual—read, write, and speak fluent Spanish.
- Experience as leader of college organization.
- Office skills include: 10-key by touch, type 48 WPM, and work well on team projects.
- Industrious and dependable—missed only one school day in the last year.
- Quick learner—able to grasp instructions accurately and complete tasks as requested.

WELL ORGANIZED

How should you organize the material on your résumé? We'll bet you can already answer that question—*the most important information related to the position you are seeking appears at the top of the page.* Ninety-nine percent of the readers of this book should have résumés that are **one page** in length. You will recall that the sections of a résumé are normally as follows:

- HEADING (your name address, etc., centered one inch from top of page)
- OBJECTIVE/FOCUS (on third line below last line of heading and usually at left)
- QUALIFICATIONS
- EDUCATION (sometimes education and employment appear in reverse order)
- SKILLS (if applicable to your résumé)
- LICENSE/S & CERTIFICATION/S (if applicable)
- EMPLOYMENT
- ORGANIZATIONS/ACTIVITIES (if applicable)

This format is considered to be professionally appropriate and will normally be used. There are many variations of this format. You will see a few examples in the Appendix that, although very similar to the format above, will have a slightly different appearance. They illustrate how the appearance and content of a résumé may vary a bit after you have a number of years of experience. You may also become creative in your layout or have a certified résumé writer assist in the preparation of your résumé. For now, the format presented in this text will serve you well. Your biggest challenge will be to write it with a high degree of professionalism. Do it well and you will receive more than your share of interviews.

WORD PROCESSED AND LASER/INK-JET PRINTED

There are several reasons why you will want to use a word processor. By using a word processor and saving to disk (making a copy on a floppy disk), you will have a permanent copy of your résumé to:

- modify for a specific position
- change and add to in the future as your experience/training accumulates
- retrieve from the computer and quickly, using the tools available on most word processors, make your résumé and accompanying materials look up-to-date.

Also it is strongly suggested that you use a laser or ink-jet printer, rather than a dot matrix, to provide printing quality that has a professional look. If you don't have one with your PC at home, make a copy on disk and go to your local copy store and ask them to print it using a laser printer.

ERROR FREE

There should be NO SPELLING, TYPOGRAPHICAL, GRAMMATICAL, OR PUNCTUATION ERRORS on your résumé! The way to avoid this is to use the tools on the word processing program, have several knowledgeable friends and teachers review it, and ask a potential employer to review the résumé and make suggestions for improving it. When you ask a prospective employer to review it, you are asking this employer for help without putting any pressure on him/her for a job. This is a good way to network with possible employers without putting demands on them. Good writing comes from rewriting many times. Write it, sleep on it, and then rewrite again and again. It takes time, but the result will be well worth it.

Remember, employers use résumés to determine the qualifications that you possess, but they also use résumés to *screen out* candidates whom they think will not make good employees. One way they do this is to eliminate those who make spelling, typographical, grammatical, and punctuation errors in their application materials. Notice the words *application materials*. You can prepare a great résumé, but if you make a glaring mistake in spelling in the cover letter, employment application, or other preliminary employment documents, it will be a very negative factor.

BRIEF: ONE PAGE

Yes, keep it short. Your authors write résumés daily for professional people with 1 to 35 years of experience and most of these résumés are one page in length, occasionally two. If professional people with this much experience can get the essentials down on one page, we are sure that most readers of this guide can also confine their résumé to one page.

Employers are busy, often reviewing 30, 40, or 100 résumés for an open position. When they receive large numbers of résumés, they spend only a very short time looking at each candidate's qualifications. Thus, if you have your best "stuff" in the qualifications section of your résumé and it appears near the top on a one-page résumé, it stands the best chance of being noticed.

SPECIFIC STATEMENTS REGARDING ACCOMPLISHMENTS/SKILLS

Do you know what the word "fluff" means? Used to describe résumé contents fluff means the résumé contains a lot of generalizations, but very few specifics. Employers want to see *specific accomplishments or skills* stated in the résumé. The following are examples of the "right way" and the "wrong way" to list accomplishments in the qualifications section of a résumé:

Right Way
- Graduated 7th in a class of 60, and was named "Outstanding Interior Design Student" in 1999.

- Knowledgeable regarding air conditioning/heating installation, maintenance, troubleshooting, controls, ducting, and systems balancing.

- Experience using Windows 95, Lotus 1-2-3, Excel, WordPerfect, and Famous Bookkeeping software.

- Completed 6 years of formal Spanish training—speak, read, and write fluently.

- Excellent communications and human relations skills—completed Dale Carnegie Course in 1999.

Wrong Way
- Received many honors during my college program.

- Possess substantial skills regarding air conditioning and heating appliances.

- Am familiar with most types of PCs and software.

- Bilingual—speak Spanish.

- Get along well with staff at store.

STYLE

Style refers to the way you write or present your qualifications in the résumé and other marketing documents which you prepare. You will note that all the examples of résumés that appear later in this chapter are one page long. They are written with brevity to maximize "punch." In other words, they are written to show your strengths in the least amount of space and in very few *action*-oriented words—words indicating achievement or active participation in projects in work-related activities.

How does one write with punch? First, you write using the first person "I"—but you assume or imply the pronoun "I" in your statements regarding your qualifications, employment, etc., you do not actually write "I" in the statement. For example, Rafael Cortez's résumé appearing in Figure 1, Chapter 1, states, "Associate Degree and Certificate in Business Office Occupations." What is assumed or implied in the qualifications statement is that the résumé writer has an Associate Degree and Certificate in Business Office Occupations. Since the style for résumés should be *brief* and written in *first person*, rather than say, "I have an Associate Degree and Certificate in Business

Office Occupations," the writer simply *implies* the "I have an" portion of the sentence by writing only, *"Associate Degree and Certificate in Business Office Occupations."* This style of writing takes a little practice but it is not difficult.

Action words are verbs that communicate *positive acts* (action) and achievement on your part. In the same Figure 1 résumé in Chapter 1, the following appears in the employment section of Rafael Cortez's résumé:

- Completed 5-month internship in busy administrative office.
- Prepared correspondence and newsletter using MS Word.
- Assisted in data entry, scheduling appointments, routing phone messages on multi-line telephone system.
- Translated for Spanish-speaking parents.
- Performed filing tasks—alphabetical and numerical.

Note that all of the bulleted items begin with action words: *completed, prepared, assisted, translated,* and *performed.* These are all words showing positive action and achievement on the writer's part. In writing résumés and cover letters, it is best to use, in addition to those above, action words such as:

achieved	*reduced*	*created*
earned	*trained*	*customized*
initiated	*organized*	*implemented*
increased	*presented*	*designed*
improved	*evaluated*	*installed*
planned	*produced*	*built*
originated	*arranged*	*promoted*

Omitting articles is also essential in good résumé writing. Articles are: *the, a,* and *an.* They are omitted primarily to keep your résumé brief and to the point. Note the following example from Cortez's employment section above, which contains no articles.

- Completed 5-month internship in busy administrative office.

In normal writing, we would write it as follows: *I* completed *a* 5-month internship in *a* busy administrative office. But to give it punch and keep it brief, the *I* and the two *a*'s were omitted.

SAMPLE RÉSUMÉS: EISCHEN'S SIMPLIFIED FORMAT

The examples of résumés for career-entry applicants that follow are intended to illustrate the qualities of the simplified résumé format discussed earlier. Check these sample résumés for the key qualities of a résumé: *attractive appearance, well organized, word processed, laser/ink-jet printed, error free, one page in length,* and *specific regarding accomplishments/skills.*

Figure 3   Marketing Assistant

Ramona E. Brooks

1218 E. Montecito, Apt. 19
Fresno, CA 93707
(559) 225-0404

OBJECTIVE

MARKETING ASSISTANT POSITION

QUALIFICATIONS

- Associate Degree in Business Administration, Marketing emphasis.
- Three years of customer service experience.
- Computer skills: PowerPoint and Presentations software, keyboarding speed: 50+ WPM, Word-Perfect, and Lotus 1-2-3.
- Excellent problem-solving ability; work well under pressure; and creative in use of computer graphics and freehand drawing.
- Team player; interact well with coworkers and management–completed courses in human relations, communications, and supervision.
- Accounting and bookkeeping skills: payroll, accounts payable/receivable, payroll taxes, bank deposits, and reconciliation of bank accounts.

EMPLOYMENT

Cosmetic Counter Manager   1998 to Present
J. C. PENNEY, Fresno, CA
- Earned "All Star" award for consistently meeting or exceeding monthly and yearly quotas.
- Plan and implement special promotions which include flyers, advertising copy, and displays.
- Process orders, product returns, and resolve customer service concerns.

Payroll Assistant   1996 - 1998
Twelfth Street Courier Service, Everett, Mississippi
- Utilized computer accounting system to prepare payroll, accounts payable/receivable, and bank reconciliation.

EDUCATION

Associate of Arts Degree in Business Administration, 1999
Fresno City College, Fresno, CA

Maintained 3.2 GPA while working full time
Earned 100% of living and education expenses

Activities: • Alpha Gamma Sigma (Fresno City College Honor Society)
             • Treasurer, Students in Free Enterprise (SIFE)
             • Volunteer, Ronald McDonald House

Figure 4 Dental Hygienist

KRISTEN A. KHAM, RDH

9619 N. Pineapple Way
San Francisco, CA 93786

(408) 299-1798
kakham@sfusanfran.edu

FOCUS

*CAREER DENTAL HYGIENIST POSITION REQUIRING DEDICATION TO
PREVENTIVE DENTISTRY, STRONG INTERPERSONAL SKILLS,
AND EXPERIENCE IN A DENTAL PRACTICE*

QUALIFICATIONS

- Associate of Science Degree in Dental Hygiene and licensure/certification for local anesthesia, radiation, curettage, dental assisting, and CPR.
- Dental hygiene experience (more than 1,000 hours) in clinical setting where full range of prophylaxis and patient care was provided.
- Prior experience as Back Office Dental Assistant: assisted in general dentistry practice preparing setup and breakdown of operatories, cements, crown preparation, and provided post-operative care.
- Commended for demonstrating initiative in back office duties; subsequently received year-end bonus.
- Excellent human relations/people skills–completed communications and team-building seminar for enhancing relationships with patients and peers.

EDUCATION

Associate of Science Degree, Dental Hygiene 1999
San Francisco City College
San Francisco, California
   Honors:
      Dean's Medallion Award (placed in top 10% of graduating class)
      Dean's List: 3.81 GPA on 4.0 scale

EMPLOYMENT

Dental Hygiene Clinical Practice, 1,000 Hours 1999
San Francisco City College Dental Hygiene Clinic
San Francisco, California

Dental Assistant, Back Office (part-time) 1996 - 1998
Harold P. Martin, DDS
- Assisted with general dentistry procedures: extractions, crown preparation, setup and breakdown of operatories, patient post-operative care, and patient education.

PROFESSIONAL LICENSES/CERTIFICATES/AFFILIATIONS

California Board of Dental Hygiene License
Dental Radiology License
CPR Certificate
Dental Assisting Certificate

Local Anesthesia, Nitrous Oxide and Curettage
  Certified
American/California Dental Hygienists' Association
Bay Area Dental Hygienists' Association

Figure 5   Brake/Front End Specialist

LOLO E. CONTRERAS

4545 W. Martin Luther Blvd.
Selma, CA 93786
(559) 297-7274

OBJECTIVE

BRAKE/FRONT END SPECIALIST, CAREER POSITION

QUALIFICATIONS

- Brakes, Suspension, and Steering Certificate awarded, 1999.
- Completed 600 hours of hands-on training in:
  Alignment (Thrustline & Total Four-Wheel)
  Power Drum and Disc Brakes, plus introduction to ABS theory
  Suspension and Steering Repair, CV Boot/Joint Service, and Axle Maintenance
- Received instruction regarding precision measurement, fasteners, gaskets, tubing, wiring, friction and anti-friction bearings, work orders, and cost/job estimating.
- *Equipment used in training included:*
  Hunter J-111
  Computerized off-the-car balancers
  On-the-car balancers
  AMMCO Drum and Rotor Lathe
  Specialty tools and hydraulic presses

EDUCATION

Certificate of Completion, Brakes, Suspension, & Steering   1999
Vocational Training Center, Fresno City College
Fresno, California
- Completed certificate program 4 weeks ahead of schedule.
- Received instructor's recommendation upon completion of program.

EMPLOYMENT

Brake Service Specialist (Part-time)   4/98 - Present
Elmer's Superior Brake Service
Fowler, California
- Employed weekends and evenings while completing brake and suspension training.
- Began at minimum wage and received two hourly wage increases while employed here.
- Work includes servicing brakes and suspension systems of commercial vehicles and farm equipment.

AFFILIATIONS

Member, Fresno County Automotive Repair and Mechanics Association
Member, Classic Chevrolet Car Owners' Association

Figure 6 Hair Stylist

ROBIN S. ANDERSON

7777 N. Pine Road
Denver, Colorado 83722
(440) 222-4390

FOCUS: HAIR STYLIST POSITION

QUALIFICATIONS

➤ Colorado State Board licensed Hair Stylist with training in *Pivot Point, Block* and *Basic* hair cutting techniques.

➤ Attended additional training seminars and received certificates in current styling and hair coloring techniques.

➤ Skilled in basic salon organization and sterilization practices.

➤ Professional appearance, positive attitude and outgoing personality. Effectively interact with clients and staff.

➤ Dependable team member who is always willing to assist other stylists.

EDUCATION

Graduate, Cosmetology Program - Hairstyling / Pivot Point System
Mountain College of Cosmetology, Denver, Colorado, January, 1998

LICENSE

Cosmetology License, Hair Styling
State of Colorado Board of Barbering and Cosmetology, June, 1998

CERTIFICATES

Hair Color Techniques '98, Matrix Products, January, 1998
Contemporary Hair Styles for Working Women, Gary Gerard, June, 1998
Perms, Cuts and More, Peter Hantz, December, 1997

EMPLOYMENT HISTORY

Receptionist/Appointment Desk
"ALL THAT STYLE" SALON, Denver, Colorado   1996 - 98
• Greeted clients, scheduled appointments and received payments for services in full-service salon.

Customer Service Representative
MOUNTAIN YELLOW PAGES, Denver, Colorado   1994 - 96

Figure 7   Bookkeeper/Accounting Clerk

GUDDI P. DHILLON

9118 Lumont St., #104
Vancouver, WA 81729
(415) 612-4187

OBJECTIVE
CAREER POSITION AS BOOKKEEPER/ACCOUNTING CLERK

QUALIFICATIONS
- Associate of Science Degree in Accounting
- Completed 34 units of accounting which include: *Computer Accounting, Tax and Auditing, and Cost Accounting*
- Performed all bookkeeping functions for 85-unit apartment complex while attending school full time.
- Experienced in converting manual bookkeeping system to computer applications without downtime or significant problems.
- Knowledgeable regarding:
  Accounts payable/receivable
  General Ledger Entries
  Financial Statements
  Quarterly and Annual Payroll Tax Reporting
  Obtaining credit information from prospective tenants

EDUCATION
Associate in Science Degree in Accounting   May, 1999
Vancouver Central College
Vancouver, WA
   GPA: 3.7 on a 4.0 scale
   Dean's List, 3 semesters
   Member, Accounting & Finance Fraternity

SKILLS
- Familiar with accounting and spreadsheet software (Lotus, Excel, Peachtree).
- Operate 10-key by touch.
- Well organized—complete projects accurately and in timely manner.
- Good listener and able to follow directions with minimum follow-up.

EMPLOYMENT
Bookkeeper/Assistant Manager   1998 - Present
Sea Cliff Apartments
Vancouver, WA
- Prepare payroll, bank deposits, financial statements, tax reports, and period-end reports.

EXERCISE III

Your Initial Draft

On the following two pages please complete the simplified résumé format by filling in the appropriate information using Exercises I and II from Chapters 2 and 3. It is suggested that you initially write out a draft of your résumé on this and the next page. However, if you have a computer available, prepare the initial draft on your word processor. It will save you the time of having to transfer the information later. Let's begin:

(HEADING)

(YOUR NAME)_____

(Address)_____

(City, State) _____

(Phone) _____

(E-mail)_____

OBJECTIVE

_____

_____

_____

QUALIFICATIONS

_____

_____

_____

_____

_____

_____

_____

_____

_____

_____

EDUCATION

_____

_____

_____

_____

_____

_____

_____

SKILLS

_____
_____
_____
_____
_____
_____
_____

LICENSES & CERTIFICATIONS

_____
_____
_____
_____
_____
_____

EMPLOYMENT

_____
_____
_____
_____
_____
_____
_____
_____
_____
_____
_____
_____

ORGANIZATIONS & ACTIVITIES

_____
_____
_____
_____
_____

Practice Your Skills

Your Name
Your Address

OBJECTIVE

QUALIFICATIONS

EDUCATION

SKILLS

EMPLOYMENT

Practice Your Skills

Your Name

Your Address

OBJECTIVE

QUALIFICATIONS

EMPLOYMENT

EDUCATION

Practice Your Skills

YOUR NAME

Your Address   Your Phone Number

FOCUS

QUALIFICATIONS

EDUCATION

EMPLOYMENT

PROFESSIONAL LICENSES/CERTIFICATES/AFFILIATIONS

Staging: Types of Résumés

INTRODUCTION

As you are probably aware, résumés, like most things in our life, are constantly changing because of technology. Today, many large employers use a process known as scanning résumés. This means the employer, upon receipt of your résumé, uses a computer-related machine to scan and store your résumé. It is also very common for a prospective employer to ask you to either fax or e-mail your résumé. And as your career progresses, you may need to change the format of your résumé slightly. After you have ten years of experience, it would be advisable to emphasize the experience section of your résumé to a greater extent. The type of résumé format that places more emphasis on your work history is called a *chronological* résumé. Should you wish to change career fields after ten years, you may need to develop what is termed a *functional* résumé, a résumé that emphasizes skills, rather than work history. Both of these types of résumés are discussed and/or illustrated on the following pages.

SCANNABLE RÉSUMÉS

Using a scanner (computer-related hardware that reads a sheet of paper and places it in computer storage) is a method that employers who recruit large numbers of new employees each year use to quickly read and store quantities of résumés. Thus, the term "scannable résumé" has originated in the last few years—meaning a résumé that is prepared in a format ready to be scanned into a computer.

If you are submitting your résumé to very large corporations like General Motors, Sears Roebuck, PG&E, Coca-Cola, Circuit City, Kaiser Permanente, or Intel Corporation, it will probably be scanned. It will be processed by a machine that will place it, along with hundreds or thousands of other résumés, in a database. When a department within the company needs a particular position filled, the database is searched for key skills or characteristics needed in the position to be filled. The search is conducted by the computer hunting for *keywords* in the résumés that are in the database. If the position to be filled is that of a machinist, in addition to the word *machinist*, keywords such as: *tool and die, set-up and operate conventional and special-purpose machines, fabricate metallic and nonmetallic parts, blueprints, specifications, determine tolerances of finished workpiece, cutting tools, mills, lathes, jig borers, grinders, shapers, micrometers, height gauges, and gauge blocks, number of years of experience, training on certain manufacturer's equipment (Cincinnati Vertical with auto-feed), schools attended,* and *address* where applicant lives may all be part of the keyword search of the résumés on file. If your résumé has the skills and characteristics required for the job, it will be identified as one that might be further screened to determine whether your qualifications are a good match for the position to be filled. The résumé will then be printed out and sent to the department needing the machinist. If it looks like a good match to the supervisor of the department, you may receive a call to come in for an interview. When this occurs, you should bring a presentation copy (a professional-looking copy as discussed and illustrated in the previous chapter) of your résumé, updated if appropriate, with you.

Additional Tips on Preparing a Scannable Résumé

Your résumé should always contain a qualifications section. In a résumé to be scanned, however, it is best to focus on placing words in the qualifications, skills, and employment sections of your résumé that are commonly used and referred to in your occupational area, like the ones referred to above for a machinist. Some résumé writers even suggest using a "keywords" section. The main thing is to do your homework. Find out the kinds of products, software, equipment, skills, and procedures that are commonly used in your occupation. Then be sure to list them either in the qualifications, skills, or employment section of your résumé. The scanning computer will pick them out regardless of where they appear in the résumé.

It is best to:

- Use white or a light-colored paper.
- Use a True Type Windows font such as Arial or Times New Roman, point size 10 to 14.
- Avoid using graphic lines, boxes, graphics, underlining, italics, and special symbols (solid bullets are OK).
- Avoid placing items in columns or using the "flush right" feature.

FAXING RÉSUMÉS

There may be a need to fax your résumé to a prospective employer. The employer may telephone and ask you to fax your résumé immediately. If this is the case, and you don't have a fax machine available, go to a local print/mailbox shop, supermarket, or drugstore. Most of these have fax machines for hire, at a cost of approximately one dollar per page. Again, a résumé that is on white paper will fax with a cleaner look. After you have sent the fax, send a copy of your professional-looking résumé on good quality paper via the U.S. Postal Service.

E-MAIL AND INTERNET RÉSUMÉS

There may be an occasion when you want to attach your résumé to an e-mail message being sent via the Internet to a prospective employer. Or, you might want to post your résumé to some of the job banks or databases that are accessible to employers on the Internet. To do either of these tasks, the procedure is to *attach* a word processing file containing your résumé to the e-mail message. However, before you attach your résumé, there are three things that need to be done:

- Format your résumé so that it can easily be transmitted via e-mail and will appear at its destination in the same format as you sent it. To do this you need to remove all the frills from the résumé. This means *all the bold, italics, underlines, bullets, tab stops*, etc., should be deleted from your résumé. When you remove all these frills, the résumé often becomes longer and may require two pages. Don't be concerned about the length; when sent by e-mail length is immaterial.

- Résumés prepared for placement on the Internet are combined with thousands of other résumés and stored in computers. When a company needs someone for a specific position, the computer database is searched looking for specific candidates by job title and skills. It is essential that you have one to three specific job titles or positions appearing at the top of your résumé, *above your name*. Thus, as in the example which follows (Figure 8), the job title *Marketing Assistant* should appear first on the page in order to be quickly noted when a computer search is conducted.

- Next, you will need to save this revised (very plain) résumé in a separate file and in a different type of file format in your word processing program. When you want to save this revised document, you should press "Save as" on your word processor and then select "ASCII DOS Text" as the format in which to save it. We also suggest you rename the file using a name that reflects it is your "very plain" e-mail/ASCII résumé. You will then send this renamed file as an attachment to your e-mail.

After you make the changes to the résumé, it will look like the résumé on the following page (Figure 8). This is the same sample résumé that appeared on page 28 in Chapter 4.

Figure 8   E-mail/ASCII

MARKETING ASSISTANT POSITION

RAMONA E. BROOKS
1218 E. Montecito, Apt. 19
Fresno, CA 93707
(209) 225-0404

QUALIFICATIONS

Associate Degree in Business Administration, Marketing emphasis.

Three years of customer service experience.

Computer skills: PowerPoint and Presentations software, keyboarding speed: 50+ WPM, WordPerfect, and Lotus 1-2-3.

Excellent problem-solving ability; work well under pressure; and creative in use of computer graphics and freehand drawing.

Team player; interact well with coworkers and management–completed courses in human relations, communications, and supervision.

Accounting and bookkeeping skills; payroll, accounts payable/receivable, payroll taxes, bank deposits, and reconciliation of bank accounts.

EMPLOYMENT

Cosmetic Counter Manager
1998 to Present
J. C. PENNEY, Fresno, CA
Earned "All Star" award for consistently meeting or exceeding monthly and yearly quotas.
Plan and implement special promotions which include flyers, advertising copy, and special displays.
Process orders, product returns, and resolve customer service concerns.

Payroll Assistant
1996 - 1998
Twelfth Street Courier Service, Everett, Mississippi
Utilized computer accounting system to prepare payroll, accounts payable/receivable, and bank reconciliation.

EDUCATION

Associate of Arts Degree in Business Administration, 1999
Fresno City College, Fresno, CA

Maintained 3.2 GPA while working full time
Earned 100% of living and education expenses

Activities:
Alpha Gamma Sigma (Fresno City College Honor Society)
Treasurer, Students in Free Enterprise (SIFE)
Volunteer, Ronald McDonald House

CHRONOLOGICAL/FUNCTIONAL STYLE RÉSUMÉS

In discussing résumés and how they should appear, you may hear or be asked if your résumé is in a chronological or functional format. The authors are not so concerned about your remembering these terms. However, if you are taking a course in résumé writing, your instructor may want you to know these terms and the difference between each of these formats.

A *chronological* résumé is one that emphasizes your employment history by date. It is actually organized in *reverse* order with your last job appearing first. Thus, the term *chronological* here means that your former jobs appear in reverse order, according to dates of employment.

This type of format is used if you have a substantial employment background and have remained in the same occupation. For example, assume you began work right out of school as a plumber and have been in that occupation for 15 years. Now assume that the company you have worked for has been sold and you need either to reapply or seek work elsewhere. In this instance it would be best to use a chronological résumé format for your résumé because long-term employment in the same occupation is considered a strength. In essence, *after stating your objective and qualifications* in the résumé, you should list your employment in reverse chronological order.

What about the *functional résumé* format? This type of format is used when you don't have a long work history or you are moving into a different occupational area. Using the example above, if after 15 years as a plumber you have decided to seek employment as a forest ranger, you need to have something more going for you than 15 years of plumbing experience. You may have been going to school at night to study forestry management and zoology, and have joined the Sierra Club. And maybe you have been a scout master or a hiker who has explored significant mountain ranges and other National Forest preserves. In this case you would state your education, experience, and activities that relate to employment with the forest service *after the objective and qualifications section of your résumé*.

Both types of résumé formats focus on putting your best qualifications nearest the top of the résumé, and remembering to list only the skills, education, knowledge, and qualifications that are important in qualifying you for the job you are now seeking.

Supporting Cast

Selling or marketing your talents is the major thrust of *all* the material you prepare when submitting a résumé. Additional materials are frequently submitted with the résumé. These include the cover letter, reference sheet, salary history, and attachments—sometimes referred to as a portfolio or addendum to the résumé. The attachments are often used to provide examples or illustrations of your work. Some occupations that often require attachments or portfolios showing samples of work are modeling, graphic arts, photography, writing, acting, or cabinetmaking. Ask an instructor or professional in your field if it is appropriate to send examples or photographs of your work with the résumé.

COVER LETTER

The cover letter is a very important part of your initial communication with a prospective employer. It should:

1. Be directed to a specific individual if possible.
2. Be well researched and written—focused on the specific requirements of the position for which you are applying.
3. State only your very best qualifications.
4. Request a meeting/interview with the potential employer.

Cover letters are usually one page in length, have the same heading as the résumé, and are written in a more formal style than the résumé. The heading should begin one-half inch, on the 4th line, from the top of the paper. Many employers read the cover letter first and will not bother to look at the résumé if the cover letter is poorly written. The next chapter will discuss and provide several examples of cover letters.

REFERENCES

Employers often request a list of references to gain information regarding your professional skills and character. You need to contact at least four people and ask each of them if they will act as an "enthusiastic" reference for you. You will want to contact them before you submit materials to potential employers so that your references will be prepared when someone calls or writes asking about you.

Who should the references be? Who knows you well enough to comment on your professional abilities and character? Probably it will be teachers, employers (supervisors), counselors, long-time friends, and respected members of the community. It is best to have one from each of these categories. Be careful not to have all teachers or all friends. And be sure to include one or two supervisors, past or present.

How do you exhibit your references? Use the same heading that appears on your résumé. Then, three lines below the last line of your heading, center the word **REFERENCES**. Four lines below, type each of your references in turn. Be sure to include the *name, title* (Miss, Mrs., Ms., Mr., Ph.D., M.D., R.N.,) *occupation*, (Sales Manager, Congressman, Business Owner) *addresses* (work location preferably), and *phone numbers* of the people who are prepared to say positive things about you professionally and personally.

You should submit your reference page to a prospective employer when you are scheduled for the first interview. Do not send it with the cover letter and résumé. The references and most special attachments should be given to the interviewer at your initial meeting unless there was a request to submit them at an earlier time.

On the facing page you will see an example of a reference page for Rafael Cortez.

Figure 9 References

Rafael E. Cortez

5559 E. Spruce Ave.
Clovis, CA 93611
(559) 845-9621

REFERENCES

Mr. Bradley Brownswager   (559) 430-4677
Owner, Bargain Mart
1219 N. Glenn St.
Fresno, CA 93722

Mr. Armando Martinez   (559) 875-8023
Teacher, Washington Union High School
1650 Lincoln Ave.
Selma, CA 93657

Mr. Phillip P. Lau   (559) 875-2190
Area Counsel: Peabody Trucking
10790 W. Shaw Ave., Suite A
Fowler, CA 93709

Ms. Mercedes Johnson   (559) 224-1700
Supervisor, IRS District Office
1240 Butler Ave.
Fresno, CA 93722

Your Name

Your Address

REFERENCES

Name   Phone #

SPECIAL ATTACHMENTS

Let's assume you want to apply for a position as a cabinetmaker or a furniture refinisher. One of the things that might impress a potential employer is the quality and creativity of your work in building or refinishing cabinets. Therefore, if you were to include with your résumé a portfolio (sample) of drawings (two or three) and several photographs of finished projects, it would permit a potential employer to view the type of cabinets/furniture that you have designed/refinished and how the end result looks in the color photographs you enclose.

Special attachments illustrating your capabilities are an effective means of communicating your talents. Candidates who provide examples of their work often stand out when compared to other applicants. Frequently, employers receive work samples from only a few candidates.

How should someone present samples or exhibits of their work? Any work that is presented should be placed on paper with your letterhead (same as the résumé) or at least have a cover sheet attached with your letterhead on it. The main thing is that all work be labeled and have a professional appearance.

SALARY HISTORY

Most individuals seeking entry-level positions and who recently completed their schooling will not be asked to present a salary history. In the event that you are asked to provide a salary history now or at some time in the future, it should be done in the format described below:

1. Use the same heading as you used on the résumé, cover letter, and references.
2. List your most recent employment and salary, and then in reverse order list previous work history—providing compensation for previous jobs for up to 10 years.

Please note the example on page 48. In this example it is assumed that Rafael Cortez has 10 years of experience in retail merchandising and account sales.

Figure 10 Salary History

Rafael E. Cortez

5559 E. Spruce Ave.
Clovis, CA 93611
(559) 845-9621

SALARY HISTORY

(Confidential)

J. C. PENNEY COMPANY - 20 stores, Regional Office, Fresno, California

Account Executive (9/98 to Present)*
Current: $50,000 annually
Starting: $35,000

Account Coordinator (1/97 - 9/98)
Ending: $28,000 annually
Starting: $25,000

BAILEYS - Santa Fe, New Mexico

Counter Manager (8/94 - 12/96)
Ending: $22,000 annually
Starting: $20,000

WEINSTOCKS - Sacramento, California

Counter Manager (9/92 - 7/94)
Ending: $18,400 annually
Starting: $16,500

STOCKTON MERCHANDISE CENTER, Modesto, California

Counter Manager (10/90 - 8/92)
Ending: $15,500 annually
Starting: $14,500

*Benefits (as Account Executive)

- *Bonus Based on Net Profit (Consistently $8 - 10,000 annually)*
- *Company Vehicle*
- *Fully Paid - Medical, Dental and Vision Insurance*
- *401K*
- *Incentive Thrift Plan*
- *Three Weeks Paid Vacation*

Practice Your Skills

Your Name
Your Address

SALARY HISTORY
(Confidential)

Company and Position   Salary

EXERCISE IV

References

Below list the names of four individuals that you will ask to act as references for you. Remember to select individuals you know from work, school, or activities within the community.

After getting their permission to use them as a reference, be sure to verify the spelling of their name, title, place of employment, and correct address and telephone number. When you make this request, it is a good idea to give them a current copy of your résumé. If they are asked to complete a reference request submitted to them by a potential employer, your résumé will help them provide accurate information.

Reference One:
1. Name _____
2. Title _____
3. Employer/Business _____
4. Address _____
5. Phone _____

Reference Two:
1. Name _____
2. Title _____
3. Employer/Business _____
4. Address _____
5. Phone _____

Reference Three:
1. Name _____
2. Title _____
3. Employer/Business _____
4. Address _____
5. Phone _____

Reference Four:
1. Name _____
2. Title _____
3. Employer/Business _____
4. Address _____
5. Phone _____

Now, using the format illustrated in this chapter, place the names you have written here in a file on your word processor. Be sure to use the same heading as on your résumé.

Best Supporting Role: Cover Letters

Why do we write letters to accompany our résumés and why are they called cover letters? They are written to personalize the application process. The purpose of your cover letter is to state the specific skills you have that are required for the position you are seeking—it spotlights your unique qualifications for a particular job. Because it *covers*, is placed on top of, the résumé, it is called a cover letter. It will often be the first part of your presentation to be seen by a prospective employer. You know that when you first meet others, your eyes usually focus on their face. So, put your best face on your résumé, and write a dynamic cover letter to make a great first impression.

You may recall from the previous chapter that the cover letter should:

1. Be directed to a specific individual if possible.
2. Be well researched and written—focused on the specific requirements of the position for which you are applying.
3. State only your very best qualifications.
4. Request a meeting/interview with the potential employer.

WRITE TO A SPECIFIC INDIVIDUAL

Try to direct your cover letter to a specific person. If possible, you want to get your letter/résumé into the hands of the person who will be doing the hiring. If you are asked to reply to the Human Resources (HR) department and can also find out the name of the manager who will be making the final decision, send a letter and résumé to each. Be sure the company and individual names/titles are spelled correctly.

SHOW COMPANY AND JOB KNOWLEDGE

It is best to know something about the organization to which you are applying. If it is a large company, your best bet is to conduct research regarding the firm by going to the library or on the Internet. The research librarian in most libraries will be glad to help you find information about the company. If it is a small local enterprise, you may visit the local newspaper office to find articles published about this company in the last two or three years. If nothing has been published, call the HR department or a receptionist at the firm and ask if they have a descriptive brochure or annual report available that provides an overview of the company's products and services. The company may be pleased that you inquired and gladly send you current information. The better informed you are about the business—what it does, where its plants/offices are located, number of employees, and growth pattern—the better prepared you will be to write a cover letter describing *how you fit into the company's future*. This same information about the organization will be valuable in the interview later (see Chapter 9).

In addition, you need to know the duties and responsibilities of the job for which you are applying. If you learn of a potential position through the newspaper and only a post office box is listed for replies, you may have only the information contained in the advertisement. However, if the company name is listed and there are only limited details regarding the job responsibilities for this position, it may be best to contact their HR department. Ask HR whether they have a "job announcement" sheet that could be forwarded to you. The job announcement sheet usually lists the required experience, skills, education, and knowledge needed for the advertised position.

The purpose in learning the *specific* job requirements is to enable you to respond to these skill requirements in your cover letter. If one of the requirements for a clerical position is a knowledge of WordPerfect 8 to format newsletters, you would want to include in your cover letter that you are experienced in using WordPerfect 8. Also that you have prepared a monthly newsletter for the past 18 months. In other words, when you discover the employer's job requirements, it is essential to *describe the qualifications that you possess that match those requirements*. This is the heart of a good cover letter.

INCLUDE BEST QUALIFICATIONS

What should you include in the letter? Your best qualifications! These are the *skills, knowledge, experience, education, and attitudes that most closely relate to the job requirements that were either listed in the newspaper or in the job announcement*. Will some of these also appear in the résumé? Yes. Because the letter is often the first communication read, it is OK to again highlight the qualifications you possess that relate to the job's requirements. It is also best to state in the cover letter any unique qualifications you possess that other applicants may not have. If that clerical position mentioned above requiring WordPerfect 8 is for employment with a parochial school and you have volunteered in your church's office for the past two summers, it would be good to state that you have clerical experience in a church office. Normally, one does not include religious affiliations in a résumé, but if the position is in a religious setting, experience working in a church office might be appropriate to include—unless the religious affiliations are incompatible.

REQUEST AN INTERVIEW

When ending a cover letter, it is suggested that you request an interview. This should be a positive statement, "I would welcome the opportunity to meet with you to further describe my qualifications for the clerical opening within the church's administrative offices." You might go on to say, "I can be reached at the above phone number after 2 P.M. daily, or a message may be left at the same number before 2 P.M." Another way of ending a cover letter is to state, "I will be calling you within a few days to arrange a time for us to meet and answer any questions you might have regarding my qualifications; I am excited about the opportunity to work in an office where integrity and values will be foremost."

SAMPLE COVER LETTERS

On the following pages are four cover letters. The format used in cover letters is as follows:

1. First paragraph—identifies the position for which the candidate is applying and is positive in tone.
2. Second paragraph—describes the qualifications possessed by the candidate that are needed in the position applied for—one's strongest skills and experience. The résumé should be referred to at the end of this paragraph. Sometimes an additional paragraph may be needed to elaborate on qualifications or to indicate that you have some specific knowledge required by the company.
3. Third paragraph—request an interview or state the intention to call for an interview time in the next few days.

Each one was successfully used to obtain interviews. The letters are all positive in tone and indicate qualifications the letter writer has that will be of value to the company where employment is sought. After a review of the letters, prepare a draft of a cover letter for yourself (Exercise V at the end of the chapter). *Make sure the letter states what you can do for the employer*, not what the employer can do for you.

Figure 11 Accounts Payable

PARTRIDGE GARRISON
714 Lombard Square
Oakland, CA 95361
(408) 792-1325

July 17, 1999

Human Resources Department
Hershey's Chocolate
P.O. Box 1818
Oakdale, CA 95361-0728

RE: ACCOUNTS PAYABLE POSITION, Hershey's Chocolate of California, Inc.

Please accept my résumé and consider me a serious candidate for the position of Accounts Payable Clerk. Your recent advertisement must have been written with me in mind as the experience and skills I possess are very closely aligned with those for the position you described.

I am a detail-oriented, well-organized accounting assistant who gets along well with staff members and management. As you seek a well-prepared assistant for your accounting department, please consider my qualifications:

- One year part-time experience in payroll, invoicing, and general bookkeeping.
- Account Clerk Certification, Kings River Community College, 1999.
- 10-key skills, good with figures and mathematics.
- Accounts payable, receivable and journal entry experience.
- Self-motivated, dependable employee with bilingual skills.
- Excellent ability to interact with other staff members.

I appreciate the opportunity to apply for this position and am sure that my background and skills make me a qualified candidate. I look forward to speaking with you in the near future.

Sincerely,

Partridge Garrison

Partridge Garrison

Enclosure

Figure 12   Production Mechanic

ALAN D. THOMPSON

350 N. Bates #101   •   Fresno, California 93701   •   (559) 712-7923

July 17, 1998

Union Pacific Transportation
Attn: Mr. Phillip Daniels
Director, Human Resources
1946 Flyway Drive
Sacramento, CA 97418

Re: PRODUCTION MECHANIC POSITION WITH UNION PACIFIC.

Dear Mr. Daniels:

It is with great interest that I submit my résumé for your consideration.

After talking with Mr. Mike Williams about the responsibilities of a production mechanic, I am sure my skills and energy will meet or exceed the expectations required of a Union Pacific production mechanic.

In addition to heavy equipment and hydraulic experience, my education in PLC's and AC control circuits has provided me with the ability to be cross-trained in signals. Some of the skills that I possess include:

Hydraulics	- Troubleshoot and repair of Sunstrand, Rex-Roth & Eaton hydrostatic drive systems, variable displacement closed-loop systems, and constant displacement open-loop systems.
Welding	- Experienced in stick, MIG & TIG, mild steel and stainless.
Electrical	- Repair of electrical motors and machines.
Diesel Engines	- Possess basic knowledge of diesel engines.

Please refer to my résumé for more detailed information regarding my experience, training, and education.

I look forward to meeting with you for a personal interview where I can demonstrate my professional skills and elaborate on my background.

Sincerely,

Alan D. Thompson

Alan D. Thompson

Enclosure

Figure 13 Medical Records Analyst

KATHLEEN N. CASTLE
1125 Bundy
Clovis, California 93612
(550) 325-9664

September 12, 1997

Kaiser Permanente
Staffing Services/HR Department
4785 N. First Street
Fresno, California 93726

Re: Medical Records Analyst position.

This letter is in response to your advertisement for a Medical Records Analyst. This position is of great interest to me as I am ready to transition my qualifications into a challenging medical records position with a respected institution like Kaiser Permanente.

In addition to my background as a Certified Medical Assistant, my experience and training has expanded to include medical records analysis and participation in FDA investigational studies. I am involved daily in documenting surgery studies and transmitting study data to the FDA. I possess substantial experience and education in ICD9/CPT coding and classification of diseases.

I have completed the necessary course work to become an Accredited Records Technician, and my program will be complete upon the fulfillment of my clinical hours.

Along with good decision-making ability, I am highly organized and computer proficient. I am confident of my skills and believe I am a viable candidate for this position. Please review the attached résumé for additional information regarding my training and experience.

Thank you for your consideration. I appreciate your time in reviewing my qualifications and look forward to speaking with you at your earliest convenience.

Sincerely,

Kathleen N. Castle

Kathleen N. Castle

Enclosure

Figure 14   Apprentice Cabinetmaker

MARTIN P. BROOKS
1485 N. Sussex Drive
Elmwood, Illinois 98716
(312) 864-2922

July 29, 1999

Mr. George Epstein, President
Well-Built Cabinet Systems
8671 E. Pontiac Blvd.
Chicago, Illinois 98711

Dear Mr. Epstein:

At the suggestion of Mr. James Archer, I am writing to express my interest in the position of Apprentice Cabinetmaker. Mr. Archer thought you might be interested in my background and training.

While attending Meader Technical College, I worked part-time for a lumber company where I was in charge of selling ready-made and custom cabinets for kitchen and bathroom remodeling. This experience enabled me to gain an understanding of the features customers really want in cabinets for their homes. In addition, I recently completed the Cabinetmaking Technology and Milling Program at Meader College where I studied:

- cabinet design, layout, construction (inlaying, veneering, laminates, caning), and finishing.
- reading prints, cost calculation, estimating, use and maintenance of joiners, planers, sanders, and lathes.
- furniture restoration, machine woodworking, and use of CAD software.

To put these skills to work in a respected firm such as yours is just the opportunity I am seeking. Please review the attached résumé and contact me at the above number so we can schedule a time to meet.

Cordially

Martin P. Brooks

Martin P. Brooks

Enclosure

EXERCISE V

Writing a Cover Letter

Obtain a job announcement for a position in which you are interested. This announcement can be found at the placement center of the college where you received your training, a state employment office, human resources office of a major employer within your community, or in the Sunday edition of a local or major newspaper.

Use the same heading as appears on your résumé. However, the heading for the letter should begin on the 4th line from the top of the page. The letter should be single spaced with a double space (one blank line) between paragraphs. Spacing before and after the date depends on the letter's length. The left and right margins of the letter are usually one inch, but may be greater if the letter is quite short. Remember, when the letter is finished it should look centered on the page. This is accomplished by adjusting the blank spaces between the date and the address and sometimes making the left and right margins larger (refer to examples of cover letters on the previous pages).

Write a draft of your cover letter using either a blank sheet of paper or preferably a word processor. Use the examples on the preceding pages as guides and refer to them frequently. The following steps are suggested:

1. Begin by creating a letterhead using the same heading as appears on your résumé. Make one change, the heading should begin on the 4th line (not the 7th as is normal for the résumé), thus leaving ½-inch of blank space at the top of the paper.
2. Write the current date.
3. Write the name and address of the individual or department to whom you are writing. Be sure the names are spelled correctly.
4. In writing the first paragraph, be sure to state the position for which you are applying and mention something positive about yourself or the company.
5. Write the second paragraph mentioning your best qualifications as they relate to the job for which you are applying. At the conclusion of this paragraph, mention that more details regarding your education and experience may be found in the résumé.
6. The last paragraph should politely ask for an interview.
7. Then on the second line after the last paragraph, sign off with any *one* of the following: *Sincerely*, *Cordially*, or *Respectfully*.
8. Space down four lines, three blank lines, and type your full name.
9. Space down two more lines and type the word "Enclosure." This tells the reader that you are enclosing something, your résumé.
10. Sign your name above your typed name using black ink.

Practice Your Skills

Your Name
Your Address

RE:

Please accept my résumé and consider me a serious candidate for the position of

Enclosure

Costuming: Résumé Presentation, Packaging, and Follow-Up

BY MAIL

Most of the time you will be submitting your cover letter and résumé by mail. How should you arrange the material (cover letter, résumé, and any additional information) you will be sending to a prospective employer?

As discussed earlier, the cover letter and résumé, plus any accompanying marketing materials, should be laser or ink-jet printed on ivory, gray, or white paper, 24 pound classic laid stock. What should be submitted to the employer initially? Send *only* the cover letter and résumé unless the advertisement or job announcement requests additional materials such as references, letters of recommendation, work samples, or salary history. The reason for sending only the cover letter and résumé initially is to avoid overwhelming the employer with documents while in the midst of reviewing 30 or 40 application packages. However, the exception to this rule would be to include samples or photographs of your work. If you believe your work samples are outstanding, include two or three with the initial résumé and cover letter—a picture is worth a thousand words.

For best results, submit your application materials in a *large* envelope (9 × 12 inches) so that the sheets do not have to be folded. The *cover letter should be placed on top* and the remaining material, depending on what is being sent at the time, should be placed underneath in the following order: *résumé, references, letters of recommendation, salary history, samples of your work*. Do not staple the material that you enclose within the envelope—use a paper clip. If you fax a résumé to an employer, be sure to follow up with a printed copy sent through the mail.

IN PERSON

Frequently, you are referred to a prospective employer by a college or state placement office, friend, teacher, current employer, or other source. When you first meet with the potential employer, it is essential that you have all of your personal employment information (résumé, cover letter, references, letters of recommendation, salary history, if appropriate, and samples of your work) with you. We suggest you purchase a *twin-pocket portfolio folder* (these folders measure 9½ × 11½ inches and may be purchased at most office supply stores). This type of folder has two pockets for placement of 8½ × 11-inch material, letter size, on either side when the folder is open. Purchase folders that are either dark blue or black, so that your cover letter and résumé will stand out against the dark background. Place your signed, unfolded letter on the right side of the opened folder and the résumé on the left. Any additional documents should be placed on the left underneath the résumé in the order described above. When you provide this material to an employer in an organized manner you give the impression that you are well organized and plan carefully. Thus, you will stand out and be one of the few applicants, if not the only one, to do so.

LETTERS OF RECOMMENDATION

It was suggested above to have letters of recommendation available for submission to an employer. If you have previous work experience or have served an internship, it would be advisable to ask your current and former supervisors/employers to write a letter of recommendation for you. The purpose of letters of recommendation is to show a potential employer what current or previous employers think of you. Assuming you have been a good employee, most employers will gladly write a letter of recommendation for you. Sometimes current and former employers ask you to write the letter and tell you that they will sign it.

What goes into a letter of recommendation? Usually the employer will state the position that you held, length of employment, your responsibilities in that position, and the positive qualities and initiative that you displayed while working for that firm. A sample of a letter of recommendation is given on the following page. Letters of recommendation should be given to a prospective employer at the time of the initial person-to-person contact, usually at the first interview. Of course, if the employer requested that letters of recommendation be sent with the initial application, do so.

Figure 15 Letter of Recommendation

DRAFT OF LETTER OF RECOMMENDATION

(Date)

To Whom It May Concern:

RE: RECOMMENDATION FOR YOLANDA MARIE ENCINAS

It is with pleasure that I recommend Ms. Encinas for a position of responsibility within the Oakdale Elementary School District.

Ms. Encinas has been an employee of Bank of America since 1994 when she began employment in a Fresno Branch. Currently she is employed with the Bank in its Oakdale Branch as a Customer Service Representative.

She is a very capable young woman who handles her daily tasks of public interaction, balancing and reconciling cash, using a multi-line phone system, word processing, filing, typing, and selling the Bank's services to its multi-lingual clientele in an exemplary manner. She has established a record of being dependable (seldom missing a day), very well organized, demonstrating initiative by recognizing what needs to be done before being asked, and is congenial in her relationships with clients and coworkers.

It is always a pleasure to recommend someone of Ms. Encinas' background for employment in a career position, knowing that she will make a valuable contribution to any organization with which she is affiliated. If you have any questions regarding her abilities or character, please call me at the above number.

Sincerely,

(Supervisor's signature)
(Typed name)

Practice Your Skills

DRAFT OF LETTER OF RECOMMENDATION

(Date)

To Whom It May Concern:

RE: RECOMMENDATION FOR

It is with pleasure that I recommend

Sincerely,

(Supervisor's signature)
(Typed name)

RÉSUMÉ FOLLOW-UP

Another gesture that will make you stand out in the crowd of applicants is to *follow your résumé* with either a personal phone call or a letter. This follow-up call or letter is something that most of the applicants will not do. Your authors suggest writing a second letter to an employer or contacting them by telephone to express a continued interest in the position. When you do this you indicate to the employer that you are truly interested in the position and are persistent in seeking employment with their firm. In conversations with employers that hire frequently, we have been told often that they interview and hire applicants that are *persistent*, those who demonstrate they really want the job.

When should you send the follow-up letter? One has to use some judgment in determining what is an appropriate time to wait before submitting this letter—it will vary depending on the company's practices. The rule of thumb that we suggest is to wait 10 days to two weeks, then mail a follow-up letter similar to the one on the following page. You will be pleased at the positive results from doing this.

Figure 16   Résumé Follow-Up Letter

DRAFT OF FOLLOW-UP LETTER

(your letterhead)

(date)

(inside address)

(Dear . . .)

RE: PARALEGAL POSITION

You have a résumé on file that was sent to you two weeks ago expressing interest in a paralegal position within your practice. I wanted to indicate a continued interest in this position.

Your firm is highly respected and one with which I would very much like to be associated. I believe that I can contribute to the firm's reputation by providing a standard of performance that is of the highest caliber.

I'm sure that you have many qualified applicants. However, I urge you to again review my cover letter, résumé, and letters of recommendation. In doing so, you will find that in addition to my paralegal degree and certificate, I have:

- outstanding letters of recommendation from lawyers in the firm where I interned.
- substantial experience in computerized legal research and writing (samples are available for your perusal).
- excellent computer and word processing skills (WordPerfect and MS Word).
- experience in interviewing and representing clients before administrative agencies.

Please call and allow me the opportunity to demonstrate and explain my qualifications more fully in an interview at your convenience. You will be glad you made the call.

Respectfully,

(signed)

Lee Ann Whitworth

Practice Your Skills

DRAFT OF FOLLOW-UP LETTER

(your letterhead)

(date)

(inside address)

(Dear . . .)

RE:

Respectfully,

On Stage: The Interview

TELL ME ABOUT YOURSELF

"Would you please tell me about yourself?" is one of the most feared questions asked in an interview. Should it cause you to stutter and break out in a cold sweat? No, not if you have prepared yourself for the interview. And if you haven't, it can almost end your chances of employment with that firm.

After completing the steps necessary to prepare a top-notch résumé and cover letter, you will have gathered most of the material needed for successful interviews that will result from following the strategies suggested in this text. The only thing that is left, as in most success stories, is to *prepare well for the interview*. This chapter will help you make plans for that first, second, and third interview. Yes, it does become easier with each interview.

TELEPHONE RECORDINGS

With the busy lives most of us lead, we have answering machines to take calls when we are not available. If you are seeking employment, you should have an answering device on your telephone or someone who communicates well taking messages for you. The message you leave on your machine should be *concise, contain correct grammar, be easily understood, and have no background sounds* (music, baby crying, people shouting, dishwasher running). An example of this type of message is:

> Thank you for calling. You have reached the Pavliches. Judy and Marvin are either at school or work now. Please leave a brief message and your telephone number, and we will return your call promptly.

Another similar message without identifying your name is:

> Hello, you have reached 446-8972. We are not available to come to the phone at this time. Please leave your name, number, and a brief message. We will return your call promptly.

As stated earlier, first impressions are important. Make sure your telephone message is professional in its entirety. A way to check is to have someone you respect and who is familiar with good business practices—perhaps a family member or neighbor who is in business—call your number and see if they think your message is appropriate.

WARDROBE AND HYGIENE

The rule of thumb regarding appropriate dress in an interview is to *dress as you would if you were employed in the position for which you are applying*. If you are applying for work in a business office, you would wear clothing for the interview that is similar to that worn by the people who work in that office. If there is a question about what is appropriate, it is usually best to dress a bit more conservatively than the most "far-out" person in the office or plant.

However, there are exceptions to this rule. Sometimes uniforms are worn by employees performing the job for which you are applying; sometimes one's job requires employees to appear in costume; and sometimes one's work requires wearing coveralls or a smock. In these instances, an applicant should dress as described below.

For a *female* interview applicant, the following is suggested:

1. Business dress—modest in length, neckline, color, and style; business suit or pants/skirt and a blouse are fine.
2. Stockings should complement your outfit—if the interviewer's attention is drawn to them, they are too jazzy.
3. Shoes should be clean, polished, and in good repair—usually a low heel is appropriate.
4. Nails should be modest in length and natural in color.
5. Tattoos on the arms should be covered by wearing long sleeves.
6. Minimal jewelry such as a watch, ring, plain necklace, or pin are in good taste. Do not wear more than two earrings per ear, nor should earrings be too large or long. Avoid noisy jewelry, such as clanging bracelets.
7. Undergarments should never be seen through or below one's outer clothing.
8. Clothing that is normally worn to parties, weddings, or dressy social affairs is *not appropriate* for an interview.
9. Perfume/cologne that has a slight scent and cannot be noticed more than three feet away is appropriate.
10. Makeup should be modestly applied.
11. Hair should be styled conservatively, and long, straight hair should be styled in such a way that it is not constantly being brushed back from the applicant's face.

For a *male* interview applicant, the following is suggested:

1. Clean, pressed cotton pants in a conservative color are appropriate.
2. A short-sleeved sport shirt (with a collar), pressed, tucked in, and in a color that matches or coordinates with the pants is in good taste. (Remember, more formal business dress is required if those on the job wear sport coats or suits and ties.) Any tattoos on the arms should be covered by wearing long-sleeved shirts.
3. Socks that are nearly the same color as the pants should be worn (not white athletic socks).
4. Casual shoes, leather, suede, low-top, clean, and shined are appropriate (wear dressier shoes if wearing suit or slacks).
5. Nails should be cleaned and trimmed.
6. You should be freshly shaven with hair, beard, and/or facial hair styles similar to those worn by the majority of workers in the department of the company where you are applying.

7. Use a deodorant, and if you wish, a mildly scented aftershave lotion (no strong colognes).
8. Wear minimal jewelry—a watch and one ring are OK—and modest earrings only if *commonly* worn on the job by other employees.

Often the person interviewing you will be older and more conservative than you. Thus, some of the dress or jewelry items that your friends think are cool may not be viewed the same way by the interviewer.

Obtaining appropriate clothing need not be expensive. Thrift and consignment stores frequently have good quality clothing for 20 percent of the original value. For example, one of our students recently purchased a skirt, blouse, and shoes from a thrift store. The outfit looked very professional and the total price for all of the items was only $12.

PLANNING FOR THE INTERVIEW

After you have made contact with an employer and scheduled an interview, you will need to do some preparation.

First, purchase a presentation folder (twin-pocket portfolio folder) as described in Chapter 8 to take with you to the interview. Place in the folder a copy of your resume, references, letters of recommendation, and, if appropriate, samples of your work. Be prepared to leave the folder with the employer. The additional items contained in the folder will enhance your chances of being selected for the position. In addition, by preparing this folder, you demonstrate outstanding planning, organizing, and presentation skills. You should also purchase a small notebook to take notes during the interview—as an employer may ask you to provide some additional information, for example a college transcript. When you make a note of this in your notebook, it again emphasizes your organizational ability.

Next, be sure you know the exact (building and office) location where the interview is to be held. The day before the interview, take a practice run and see how long it takes to get there—consider traffic conditions at the time the interview is planned. Plan on arriving for the interview 10 minutes before it is scheduled.

When you arrive for the interview, give the receptionist your name and tell him/her the name of the person who is expecting you (which you have memorized) and the scheduled time for your interview. Anticipate a wait longer than 10 minutes. Interviews that go well often last longer than originally expected, and so the interviewer runs past the appointed time. While waiting in the reception area before being interviewed, take out the note cards you have prepared (see next section in this chapter, Preparing for the Interview Questions) containing some of the anticipated questions and review them.

When you are called into the office to be interviewed, address the interviewer by name using Ms. Mrs., Mr., or Dr., and smile. Remember to smile frequently during the interview. Will you be nervous? Yes, of course. Does the employer expect you to be nervous? Yes. Women should offer to shake hands only if the interviewer extends his/her hand. Men should extend a firm handshake to another man, and wait to have a hand extended by a woman interviewer.

PREPARING FOR THE INTERVIEW QUESTIONS

In preparing your answers to the questions most likely to be asked, you will need information about the company that you have gathered from the library, off the Internet, or from a brochure or job announcement. The more you know about the company the easier it will be.

The *primary function of the interview is to find out if you have the skills, training, experience, and interest necessary to fulfill the requirements of the position.* Most employers are trying to determine if you will fit the job and their corporate culture (company personality). If you are hired, will it be a lasting relationship and are you going to remain with the employer for at least several years? They will ask you a series of questions to try to determine if you, the job, and the company are compatible.

What kinds of questions will they ask? On the following pages are some typical questions and responses we think are good answers—not the only answers. The questions are grouped into four categories. Remember, these are only typical responses. Your responses need to be personalized to you and your qualifications.

Some universal suggestions to those being interviewed are:

1. Smile frequently during the interview.
2. Use the name and title of the interviewer (Ms., Mrs., Mr., Dr. . . . .).
3. When you shake hands, do so firmly, grasp the entire hand, not just the fingers.
4. Wait to be asked to be seated.
5. Maintain eye contact with the interviewer (*very important*).
6. Sit up straight in the chair, don't lean on the interviewer's desk, and keep your hands still.
7. Be positive in your comments, outlook, and attitude.
8. Avoid chewing gum or tobacco.
9. It is best not to smoke or even smell of smoke during the interview—the vast majority of employers/employees don't smoke.

TYPICAL QUESTIONS REGARDING YOUR QUALIFICATIONS

Questions	**Suggested Responses**
1. Please tell me about yourself.	"I've recently completed a clerical office program at Valley Community College. I took classes and completed an internship that provided me with an understanding of medical terminology, billing, scheduling appointments, and word processing. And I have an excellent letter of recommendation from Dr. Schwartz's office where I completed my 600-hour internship."
2. What are your strongest skills?	"I believe my strongest skills are word processing, using either WordPerfect or MS Word. During my internship, I prepared correspondence, memorandums, newsletters with extensive graphics, and tables containing lots of numbers. I am also taking an advanced course in MS Word."
3. Why should we hire you?	"By hiring me you will be getting a well trained apprentice plumber with excellent skills such as the ability to work with copper, steel, cast iron, and plastic pipe; and the ability to install appliances such as heaters, boilers, and air conditioners. Also you will be getting someone who wants a career position. I was with my last employer for more than four years."

4. What do you know about this job?

"I downloaded a job description from the Internet. It indicated you were looking for someone (programmer and Network Administrator) with a knowledge of C+++, COBOL, and dBASE. I am proficient in these computer languages, plus I have LAN skills using Novell networking hardware and systems."

5. Will you please tell me about any training that relates to this job?

"I worked part-time as a clerk/cashier for Wal-Mart while I completed the Sales Associate Program at Miller Community College. The program and part-time experience taught me to make change correctly, balance a cash drawer, greet customers politely, and make suggestions for using other services that the store provided."

6. Why do you want to work for this company?

"I went to the library at school and found that Richard's Electric is one of the fastest growing HVAC firms in Wisconsin according to an article in *Business Week*. With the growth expected for this company, I see long-term opportunities and possible promotions with Richard's as a Heating & Air Control Systems Analyst."

7. Please describe your work experience.

(Same type of response as given for #5 above.)

8. Are you willing to travel in this position?

"Yes, as a single woman who would like to see more of the southwestern U.S., travel sounds great. In fact, I would welcome an opportunity to travel and even consider relocation to another state."

QUESTIONS REGARDING CHARACTER

Questions

Suggested Responses

1. How long were you with your former employers?

"All of my positions have been part-time while taking classes, except in the summer when I worked full time. I have been with my present employer for 18 months and the previous one about a year. I learned a great deal in my present job where I was given a research project where I utilized case digests, Shepard's Citations, and on-line systems such as Lexis."

2. What are your strengths and weaknesses?

"My strengths are in my ability to work as a team member, take instruction, learn quickly, and constantly look for better ways to complete assignments. Perhaps a weakness might be that I sometimes work on a project until it's perfect. I'm beginning to realize that this is not always practical from a time management point of view."

3. Do you work well under pressure?

"Yes, most of the time. While working as a teller at a credit union while going to school, we were robbed by a gunman with a ski mask over his head. I kept my cool and followed all the procedures that we had been taught. We were complimented later by management for following proper procedures."

4. What are you proudest of?

"When I completed the Welding Program at Paramount Vocational College, I was named the "Trainee Most Likely to Succeed" by my classmates. It made me feel good that my buddies thought I would be a success as a welder."

5. What types of things irritate you about coworkers?

"Sometimes other employees goof off when they are supposed to be working and that causes me to have to do more work. I'm beginning to learn that if I do my job well and let the supervisor handle employees who goof off, things work out best."

6. Are you OK working for a younger supervisor?

"Yes, in fact my current boss is a woman six years younger than me."

7. Describe your best and worst bosses.

"I've not had any really bad bosses. But I have had bosses that I admire more than some of the others. The best bosses give clear instructions, let me use my initiative, are always available for questions, and tell me when I do a good job. I think I would like to be a supervisor some day."

8. What have you learned from your mistakes?

"That when I make a mistake, I should admit it and try to learn from it so that I won't make the same mistake again."

9. What do you know about this company?

"I called the Human Resources Department and they sent me a brochure and annual report that told me a lot about the company. I learned how the company was selling more than 70% of its products on the Internet and I feel my knowledge of creating home pages and HTML would be useful in this position."

QUESTIONS REGARDING CAREER GOALS

Questions

Suggested Responses

1. What do you want to be doing in in 15 years?

"I would like to be a plant maintenance supervisor. I plan to continue to take courses at the community college and within three or four years become certified by the American Plant Maintenance Association. I have enjoyed repairing, troubleshooting, and diagnosing equipment problems all my life."

2. What are your hobbies and work?

Note: Mention hobbies that relate to the type of occupation you have chosen. A follow-up response after question #1 just above for a plant maintenance position would be:
"I have quite a collection of model cars, some of which actually can be operated by remote control. Eventually I hope to restore a 1957 Chevrolet—that's kind of my dream."

3. Do you plan to continue your education?

"Yes, in fact I have signed up to take Beginning Spanish this fall."

4. What kind of work interests you most?

"Cooking. I have always been fascinated by recipes and creating special dishes for family holidays. I know this position is for a fry cook, but eventually I want to be a chef in a major restaurant."

5. What are your salary expectations for the future, say 5 years?

"I believe this position pays $1,800 per month to begin. When I complete my additional course work and demonstrate my skills and loyalty to this company, I would expect that I would be earning 25 to 40% more in five years than when I began."

6. What motivates you?

"I imagine the same thing that motivates most people: doing work I like; being able to have some control over the work that I do; receiving praise for a job well done; and being paid and treated fairly."

7. Do you consider yourself a leader or a follower?

Be honest! If you are a follower, and most people are, say something like the following:
"I'm more comfortable when others make decisions and I follow them. When I work in a team situation, I like to give my input."

8. Of the classes that you have taken, which did you like best? Why?

Naturally, this depends on your major and occupation, but the classes you indicate should be related to the type of work you want to do. An example would be:
"Advertising was my favorite class. I really enjoyed writing ads. In fact, I worked for the school newspaper and obtained advertising material from local merchants. I helped most of them with layout and copy for the ads. That was really fun."

DIFFICULT OR STRESS QUESTIONS

Questions

Suggested Responses

1. If another employee asked you to sign him/her out because he/she was leaving 45 minutes early, how would you handle this?

"I would simply tell them I wasn't comfortable doing that."

2. If your boss asks you do to some birthday shopping for her son on your lunch hour, what would your response be?

"That would be tough. I would have to think about this—how well I knew the boss, whether it was a one-time thing, what kind of sacrifice it would take on my part to do this errand, and why my boss couldn't do it herself."

3. What are your greatest weaknesses?

Never say you don't have any! No one on this planet is perfect. A better way to handle this is:
"Sometime I become impatient with coworkers because I want to get the job done on schedule, but usually I try to find out what's going on with them and try to help them so the project gets completed on time."
or
"My writing skills are not quite as good as they should be, so I am taking an English course at the Adult Education Center in Provo this summer."

4. What do you expect in the way
    of a beginning salary?

    *Tread lightly. Try to get the interviewer to give you the
    range for this job. Also be sure you have done your homework
    and have a good idea what the job "normally" pays. You can
    say:*
    "I would assume that the pay would be based upon the
    responsibilities, experience, and education of the indi-
    vidual to be hired."
    or
    "The job announcement that I received from HRD said the
    salary range was between $14 and $18 an hour."

5. Have you ever been fired from
    a job?

    Be honest and tactful.
    "No."
    or
    "Yes, once when my supervisor learned that I was looking
    for another job. But I found another job within 10 days."

6. What type of things do friends
    or family tease/criticize you about?

    "My sister is always kidding me about taking classes.
    I never seem to have the opportunity to learn all the
    things that I want to know about."

EXERCISE VI

Personalizing Answers to Typical Interview Questions

Obtain a packet of 3 × 5-inch ruled note cards. Write each question on the preceding pages on one side of a card, in turn. Then, on the reverse side, prepare
a response that is appropriate for you, your education, experience, goals, and
the position for which you will be applying. Now memorize the answers that
you prepared on the reverse side of each card. When you do this, you will be
very confident when you go in for an interview appointment. And confidence
equals success and job offers!

Questions for You to Ask

You should ask some questions during the interview and at the end. Try to
prepare a minimum of three questions to be asked during the interview.
Doing this will let the interviewer know that you are sincerely interested in
the position. Also, you can gain some valuable information about the job,
company, and supervisors from the answers to these questions. This will
assist you in deciding whether you want to work for this company when a job
offer is made. Some of the questions that are appropriate for you to ask are:

1. Could you describe in more detail the responsibilities of the job?
2. What skills are most critical in this job?
3. Is this a new position or did someone leave?
4. What type of person would be most successful in this position?
5. How is someone evaluated on their performance in this position?
6. Would it be all right for me to volunteer to come in for a day to see what
    the work is really like in this department?

7. What is the company's practice and philosophy regarding additional training?
8. When might I expect to learn of your decision about filling this position?

After the Interview

When the interview is concluded, thank the interviewer, express an interest in the position, and ask when you might learn of the decision about filling it. Shake hands, if appropriate, and leave. Smile and say goodbye to the receptionist on the way out.

Follow-Up Letters to the Interview

Within 24 hours write a thank-you letter to the interviewer. Again, completing this step will make you stand out, as most applicants don't follow up the interview with a thank-you letter. The purpose of the letter is to demonstrate courtesy, express continued interest in the position, and provide additional information regarding your qualifications that you might have forgotten to state during the interview. The follow-up letter may be handwritten or word processed. Handwrite the letter only if you have excellent handwriting. Proofread this letter just as carefully as you did your résumé.

Another thing that will make you stand out is to contact the employer again, about 10 to 14 days after the interview. The contact may be made by telephone or another letter. Either is appropriate. It demonstrates your continued interest in the position. The letter should be short and simply state your interest and willingness to return for a subsequent interview or to answer any questions by telephone. Again, if you think of any skills or qualifications that you failed to mention during the interview, state them in the call or follow-up letter.

On the next page is an example of a follow-up letter to the interview from an applicant who was applying for a position as a bookkeeper/accountant.

Figure 17   Interview Follow-Up Letter

FOLLOW-UP LETTER TO THE INTERVIEW
(your letterhead)

(date)

(inside address)

Dear Ms. _____ :

I enjoyed the opportunity to meet with you regarding the bookkeeping/accountant position that is open at Murray Equipment Supply.

One of the things that I failed to mention to you during the interview is that last summer, while I was working in Yosemite National Park as a bus driver, my supervisor asked me to keep the records and schedules for the drivers. Since my boss knew that I was studying accounting, he asked if I would prepare all of the work schedules and bus routes using a spreadsheet program with which he was unfamiliar, MS Excel. Thus, I spent about three weeks using Excel to provide worksheets for more than 40 bus routes and 16 drivers. In addition, I trained my supervisor on how to use Excel in preparing future schedules and routes.

It is exciting to be considered for the position at Murray. I do hope that you will call me if you have any additional questions regarding my qualifications and interest in the position.

Sincerely,

(signature)

(your typed name)

Practice Your Skills

FOLLOW-UP LETTER TO THE INTERVIEW

(your letterhead)

(date)

(inside address)

Dear Ms. _____ :

I enjoyed the opportunity to meet with you regarding

Sincerely,

(signature)

(your typed name)

Curtain Call: The Second Résumé

After working for a few years in the occupation for which you initially prepared, you may decide to continue your education or to seek more challenging employment with another firm. This section will discuss and provide examples of résumés for those who are attempting to obtain employment after working for a few years or who have completed a four-year degree and are seeking employment in the field in which they majored.

The emphasis for a later résumé will more than likely focus on your experience or further education. After you have entered the workforce, the primary concern of future employers will be how well you performed on your last job. Your work history becomes critical. Our suggestion is to stay with your first job for at least 18 to 24 months. This gives you enough time to gain experience, develop your skills, and demonstrate stability to subsequent employers.

For those with additional education, employers will look at the type of education, skills acquired, leadership activities, internships or employment, projects and/or research completed, and how well (grade point average, GPA) someone performed in his/her major.

PROFESSIONAL ASSISTANCE

As your career progresses and you are in need of more sophisticated job search materials, we offer a few suggestions. In our competitive society your cover letters and résumés will be competing with those of other well-qualified candidates. Make sure your job search materials are of a quality that place you above the competition and at the top of the interview list. If you decide to seek the services of someone more knowledgeable to assist you with the writing of your résumé, we recommend you obtain someone who has been *certified* (is not just an association member) by either the Professional Association of Résumé Writers or the National Résumé Writers Association.

EXAMPLES OF RÉSUMÉS FOR THE YOUNG PROFESSIONAL

Immediately following are examples of two résumés for those who are seeking a second position after having had several years of experience. On the subsequent pages are examples of résumés of those who have continued their education and received a four-year degree.

You will note that the formats used on these résumés differ somewhat from those illustrated earlier in this text. As you become more experienced, your résumé will also become more creative and complex. Its layout becomes even more important—it has to be presented in a format that will make it stand out. However, the rules discussed earlier still apply. *Place the experience, education, skills, and achievements most relevant to the position you are seeking at the very top of the résumé.*

Figure 18 Paralegal

SCOTT R. ALMADEN

3029 Pacheco Avenue
Sacramento, California 95608
(916) 560-3298

PARALEGAL

*Articulate, poised legal professional with substantial education and experience
in procedural law and research.*

SUMMARY OF QUALIFICATIONS

➤ *Areas of education and experience:* Legal Research and Writing, Discovery and Trial Preparation, Deposition Summation, Subpoena Preparation, Litigation, Law Office Practices, Torts and Contracts, Criminal Law, Business Law, and Business Organizations.

➤ *Computer skills:* IBM computer environment with Windows and WordPerfect. Experienced in performing legal research (Internet) utilizing California governmental databases.

➤ *Strengths:* Highly motivated and focused with excellent communication and organizational skills.

➤ *Languages:* Read, write, and speak fluent Spanish.

PROFESSIONAL EXPERIENCE

WEST COAST LEGAL SERVICE, San Jose, California   1998 to Present
Field Representative
- Maintain a satellite office in Fresno for service of legal documents to residents in the Central Valley.

MCCORMICK, BARSTOW, SHEPPARD, WAYTE, & CARRUTH, Fresno, California   1997 - 98
Library Clerk
- Maintained law library, ensuring that most recent cases and other legal resources were included in firm's legal collection.
- Performed limited legal research and assisted staff with word processing.

FRESNO CITY COLLEGE, Fresno, California   1996 - 98
Office Assistant - Office of Admissions and Records
- Extensive interaction with students concerning admission, financial aid, and transcripts.

DOCUMENT COPY SERVICE, San Francisco, California   1995
Field Representative
- Served legal documents for clients and maintained Fresno office for company.

EDUCATION

Fresno City College, Fresno, California
Paralegal - Certificate of Achievement, 1998

Associate of Arts Degree in Liberal Studies

Accomplishments:
Dean's List 1996 and 1998
Valley Business Conference academic scholarship recipient, Fall 1998

Figure 19 Account Coordinator

DONNA P. MENDEZ

2196 E. Sample
Fresno, CA 93710
(559) 238-8299 (Home)
(559) 924-6000, Ext. 106 (Work)

OBJECTIVE	REVLON ACCOUNT COORDINATOR

SUMMARY OF QUALIFICATIONS

- Six years of retail sales and management experience (3 years in cosmetics)
- Promoted to Counter Manager ("C" to "A" store) in my first year with Clinique
- Team player with excellent human relations skills; effectively relate to, train, and motivate consultants while maintaining high morale
- Customer focused; proven ability to generate new business & maximize customer loyalty
- Results oriented; consistently contribute to counter goals and company profits
- Commended for merchandising skills & maintaining superior counter image
- Excellent organizational and communication skills

PROFESSIONAL EXPERIENCE

WEINSTOCKS, Fresno, CA   1993 to Present
Clinique Counter Manager, Clovis Fair (1996 to Present)
- Increases in gross sales since assuming Counter Manager position include:
  - ★ *Spring '97 GWP sales increased 19%*
  - ★ *Spring '96 GWP sales increased 22%*
  - ★ *Turnaround Cream TV Week promotion sales increased 36%*
  - ★ *1997 3-Step sales at 19% (up from 17%); 1995 Turnaround Cream sales at 7% (up from previous 4%)*
- Achieved "Team Pro" award, March '97, for highest department increase
- Chosen to attend a breakfast with executives, central region representative
- Counter added a part-time consultant in Dec.'96 due to increase in business
- Additional awards include: "3-Step Increase in Sales" for Jan. & Feb. '97 and "Powder Pairs" contest (event resulted in 57% increase)

Clinique Counter Manager, Visalia (1994 - 95) (Part-time Consultant, 1993)
- Achieved "Employee of the Month" award
- Achieved 1994 Stretch Goal with a 20% increase in sales
- Spring '94 GWP achieved a 5% increase (the only Fresno store with an increase)
- Counter achieved a 70% increase in 3-Step sales in 1993

Sales Associate, Men's Furnishings (1991 - 94)
- Achieved "Employee of the Month" award (2 months)
- Contest winner, annual "Jockey Sale" (most products sold in Weinstocks' stores)

EDUCATION

Associate of Arts Degree, Fresno City College, 1991
California State University, Fresno, Fall '91

Figure 20 Research Assistant

WILMA JOHNSON

*1947 N. Pleasant
Fresno, California
93711*

(559) 436-8112

---

*Highly motivated,
creative UCLA
graduate—*

*Commended for
being conscientious
and resourceful.*

Education and skills have provided strengths in:

- HUMAN RELATIONS & COMMUNICATION
- PROJECT COORDINATION
- RESEARCH
- LEADERSHIP ABILITY

SUMMARY OF QUALIFICATIONS

➤ Effectively relate and communicate with professionals and staff at all levels.

➤ Articulate with excellent written communications skills and a bachelor's degree in English.

➤ Proven ability to learn quickly and perform multiple tasks in an expedient manner.

➤ Confident, capable, and industrious—work equally well in self-directive environment and as a team member.

➤ Bilingual in Spanish.

➤ Keyboarding skills and computer proficient in Microsoft Word, WordPerfect 8 and Windows 95 & 98.

EDUCATION

Bachelor of Arts Degree in English
University of California, Los Angeles, 1998

Achievements:
- Completed bachelor's degree in three years.
- Maintained a GPA of 3.5 while working 35 hours per week.
- Received Editor's Choice Award from the National Society of Poets.
- Published poetry in American Journal of College Poets.

Goals:
- To pursue a Master of Arts Degree in English.
- Obtain a challenging career position utilizing excellent written, verbal, and bilingual communication skills.

EMPLOYMENT

Access Control Monitor
Business Enterprises, Los Angeles, California   1/96 - 9/98
- Responsible for access security for UCLA campus residential halls.
- Received commendation for effectively managing emergency situations.

Research Assistant
Professor Hershel Whitewater, UCLA
Humanities Department   6/98 - 9/98
- Researched and compiled a database of university & community programs and classes available to authors throughout the United States.

Sales Associate
Talbot's, Fresno, California   1994 - 95
- Provided sales assistance for customers at this premier clothing store.

Figure 21 Business Systems Analyst

DAVID NISHIMOTO

3711 N. Blackstone Avenue #112
Fresno, California 93710
(209) 226-4433

BUSINESS SYSTEMS ANALYST

PROFILE

Management Background - Seven years experience in management which included cost control analysis, utilizing and maintaining computer hardware & software, POS support, inventory control, and staff training.

University Degree - Business Administration, Information Systems Degree with projects which included systems analysis, design, and implementation for local businesses; and course work in statistical and information system analysis, management and database systems, and networking.

Computer Skills - Proficient in IBM and Macintosh computer environments with Windows and DOS. *Software:* Lotus 1-2-3, Microsoft Word & Excel, WordPerfect, and PowerPoint. *Languages:* COBOL.

Strengths - Confident and well organized with strong technical, analytical, writing, and leadership skills. Excellent human relations skills with the ability to interact well with management, staff, and clients. Speak 3 languages (English, Spanish, and Japanese).

PROFESSIONAL EXPERIENCE

DR. PHILLIP PATERNO, CALIF. STATE UNIVERSITY, Fresno, California   8/96 - 12/97
Teaching Assistant,
• Assisted students in compiling and analyzing data in upper-division statistics laboratory course.

SUMMER BRIDGE PROGRAM, CALIF. STATE UNIVERSITY, Fresno, California   6/96 - 8/96
Internship, Excel Project
• Provided system support to Equal Opportunity Program Department.
• Wrote step-by-step procedural manuals for programs, installed anti-virus software, and trained students in effective utilization of the Internet.

JACK IN THE BOX RESTAURANT, Fresno, California   11/94 to Present
Assistant Manager
• Utilize and maintain computer system for inventory control, ordering, scheduling, financial/payroll records and sales reports.
• Responsible for analyzing and controlling food, labor, & paper costs, forecasting, and hiring, training, supervising, and reviewing personnel.

CARL'S JR. RESTAURANT, Fresno, California   4/90 - 11/94
Shift Leader
• Performed daily/weekly/monthly inventory control, controlled food, paper, & labor costs, and maintained employee time records & schedules.

EDUCATION

Bachelor of Science Degree in Business Administration; Information Systems emphasis
California State University, Fresno; projected completion, May, 1997

Affiliations: International Business Association

Associate of Arts Degree in Business Administration
Fresno City College, Fresno, California, 1996   Honors: Dean's List, '95 & '96

Figure 22 Accountant-Auditor

Robert Northrop

9120 North Grand Avenue #P, Covina, CA 91724, (626) 747-1133, Northbrook@aol.com

PROFILE

- Experienced in auditing and contract review of municipal entities.
- Degree in Accounting with 50% of examination requirements for CPA licensure completed.
- Initiated successful proposal for the establishment of professional resource library to be utilized by audit team.
- Active member of Institute of Internal Auditors.
- Youngest member selected to participate in Vendor's Review Committee.
- Participated in recruiting activities for hiring new Audit Division staff.

PROFESSIONAL EXPERIENCE

Accountant-Auditor   *6/97 - present*
County of Los Angeles, Audit Division
Los Angeles, CA

Auticing

- Perform compliance audits for Department of Public Social Services (DPSS).
  - Conduct interviews to ascertain department's processes/procedures relevant to the audit.
  - Prepare schedules/work papers with comments and recommendations relative to work performed.
  - Review payroll and purchasing cycles.
- Perform compliance reviews per state regulations.
  - Perform various data analyses and audit sampling to validate assessments and evaluations documentation.
  - Interview division heads to clarify pending issues relevant to validation of documentation.
- Perform cost analyses & review feasibility of Alternate Public Defender's Office.
  - Conduct cost surveys, revenue analyses, and investigations.
  - Interview presiding judges/court administrators regarding quality of service issues.

Contract Review

- Review requested proposals regarding contract language, consistency, accuracy, and pertinent accounting/auditing issues for various DPSS programs.
- Member of committee for selecting vendors to award service contract.
- Perform in-depth analytical reviews of contract cost proposals for various DPSS support programs.

ROBERT NORTHROP   **2**

Accountant   *1/97 – 6/97*
Mario Del Fante Florist
West Covina, CA

- Performed small business accounting functions.
- Assisted in the reorganization of office procedures, including updating accounting and information systems.
- Participated in financial and strategic planning of business.

SKILLS

- Proficient in MS Excel, MS Word, Windows 95, and Internet.
- Excellent writing and spreadsheet skills.

EDUCATION

Passed law and taxation/governmental portions of CPA exam, May 1998.

Bachelor of Science Degree, Accounting
University of La Verne, 1997
Cum Laude, Departmental Honors in Accounting
Major GPA 3.9

Associate of Science, Liberal Arts
Fresno City College, 1995
Graduated with Highest Honors.

HONORS & AFFILIATIONS

Member, Institute of Internal Auditors (IIA).
Alpha Chi National Honors' Society (ULV).

For Your Notes

For Your Notes

For Your Notes

For Your Notes

For Your Notes

For Your Notes